DAKS

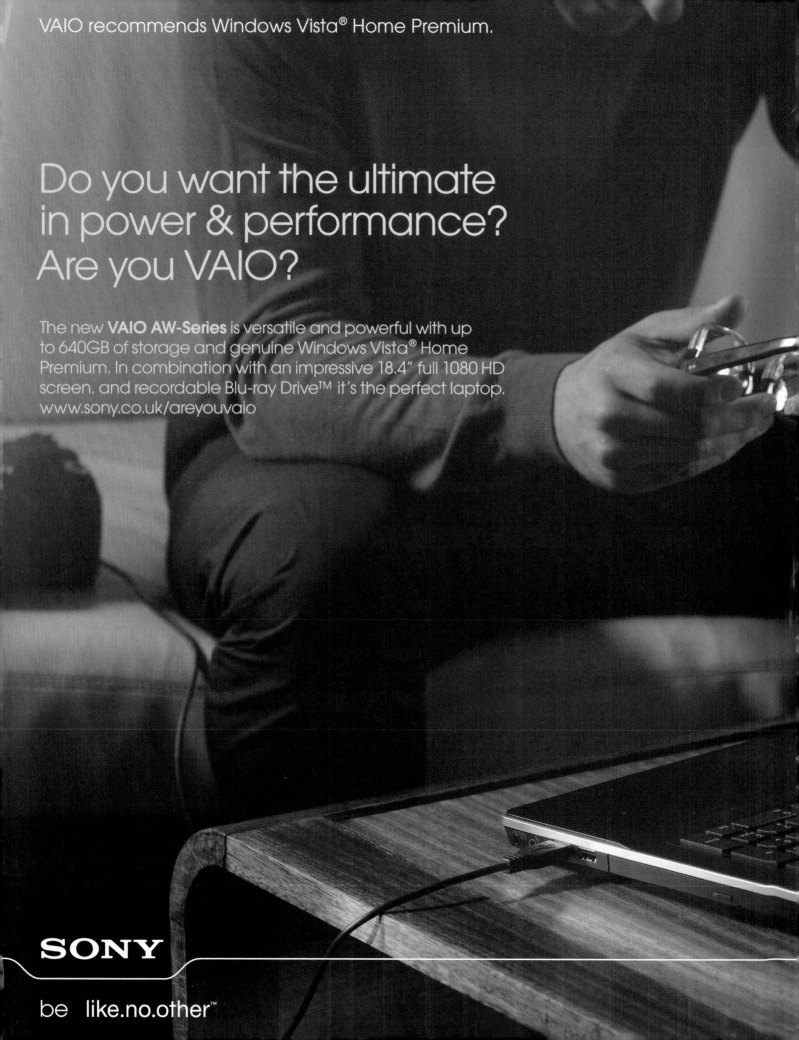

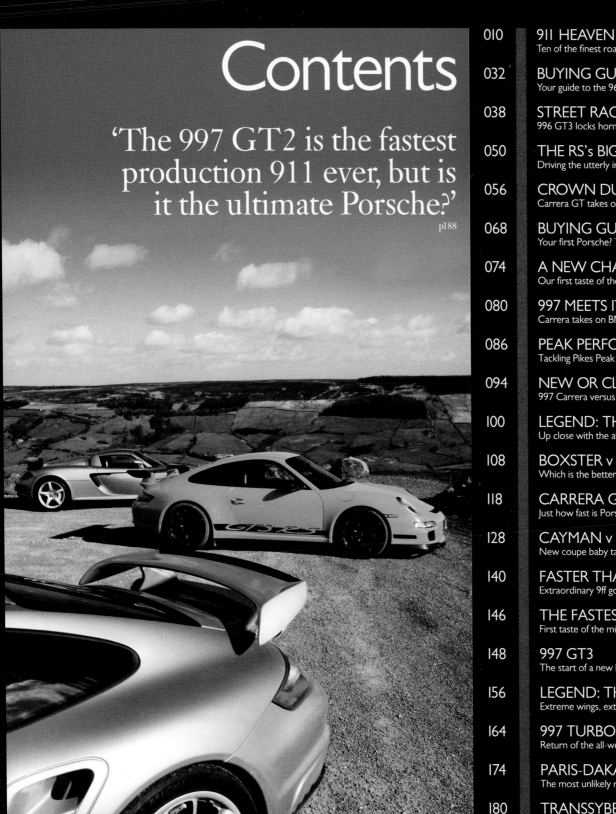

Contents

'The 997 GT2 is the fastest production 911 ever, but is it the ultimate Porsche?'

p188

Introduction

We've been teased a fair bit over the years about the number of Porsches that win **evo** group tests. It's true that they do win more than most, but there's a very good reason for that. No other marque embodies the qualities that make a great drivers' car quite so vividly or consistently as Porsche.

Of course, not everyone wants to believe it, but all it takes is a half-hour drive on a twisting B-road. No-one with an ounce of sensitivity in their fingers and backside could fail to be absorbed with the constant interaction, the intimate connection with car and road, that characterises the best of these machines. No enthusiast with a soul could remain unmoved by the unique sounds and characteristics of one of those flat-sixes in full cry.

In 2008, Porsche celebrated 60 years of road car production, and **evo** had a smaller celebration of its own as we reached our own tenth birthday. In those ten years we've been privileged to drive many great Porsches. The articles in this special bookazine celebrate many of the landmark cars that have contributed to the Porsche legend. We hope you enjoy it.

Peter Tomalin, managing editor

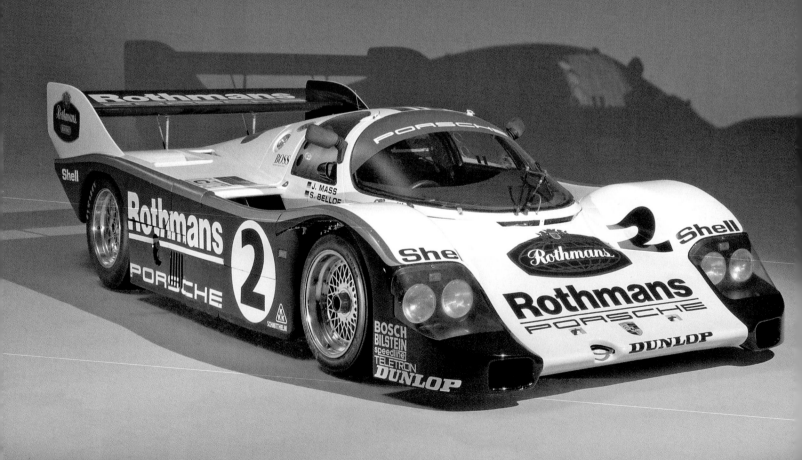

evo
MAGAZINE

Porsche Supercars
From the publishers of evo magazine
www.evo.co.uk

Editorial
5 Tower Court, Irchester Road, Wollaston,
Northants NN29 7PJ, United Kingdom
email eds@evo.co.uk
Telephone 0207 907 6310

Subscriptions
0844 844 0039

Managing Editor
Peter Tomalin

Designers
Adam Shorrock, Chee-Chiu Lee, Neil Carey

Contributing writers
Rowan Atkinson, John Barker, Jethro Bovingdon,
Brett Fraser, Roger Green, Richard Meaden,
John Simister, David Vivian

Contributing photographers
Stuart Collins, Gus Gregory, Barry Hayden,
Andy Morgan, David Shepherd, Kenny P

Advertising
30 Cleveland Street, London WIT 4JD
Email ads.evo@dennis.co.uk
Group advertising manager Des Flynn
(020 7907 6742)
Advertising director Sarah Perks
(020 7907 6744)
Deputy advertising manager Tim Deeks
(020 7907 6773)

Dennis Motoring
Editorial director Harry Metcalfe
Group publishing director James Burnay
Managing director Ian Westwood

Dennis Publishing Ltd
COO Brett Reynolds
Group finance director Ian Leggett
CEO James Tye
Chairman Felix Dennis

911

H E A V E N

Back in 2001 we gathered ten of the finest roadgoing 911s, including the then-new GT2, to find out which was the greatest of all

9 11. It's an icon, a legend, a four-wheeled testimony to the process of evolution. Few cars, let alone sports cars, have enjoyed such an extended production run and evolved so purposefully and effectively. Certainly no other car has been a match for the best in its class for four decades, and no other car has remained so compellingly desirable.

The original 911 was unveiled in 1964 and back then no-one, not even its designer, 'Butzi' Porsche, could have predicted that 911 would become such a revered number, or that the petite, curvaceous 2+2 would be pivotal to the fortunes of the company through to the next millennium. Its overhanging rear engine ought to have limited its lifespan, yet while the rest of the market subsequently abandoned the layout, Porsche famously – stubbornly almost – persevered and refined it, accentuating its advantages while gradually minimising its shortcomings.

It's a measure of Porsche's success that, 37 years later, it has no qualms about launching the new GT2, a 911 with 455bhp, rear-drive and only organic traction control – the driver's right foot. In the mid-'80s this would have seemed outrageous even within the walls of Porsche's research and development department in Stuttgart. There, its engineers had been given free rein to make the accountants weep and create what remains the most incredible 911 derivative, the 959. We're still waiting for a road car with a more sophisticated four-wheel-drive system – a system deemed necessary to handle the sledgehammer blow of the twin-turbo engine's 450bhp…

Try to explain the 911's appeal to someone who's never driven one and you keep coming back to the engine. The uniquely vocal flat-six dominates the car and it doesn't need to be gargantuanly powerful. Indeed, the less muscular, non-turbo versions of the six-cylinder horizontally-opposed 'boxer' are generally more characterful and deliver instantaneous throttle response, which you'll appreciate as you get to grips with the initially odd balance that its far flung location dictates; the nose light and bobbing along the road surface, the tail heavy and driven into it by the engine's weight.

You never forget your first hack along a twisting road in a 911 – the abundant, precisely delivered urge, the almost lazy, guttural throb that resonates through the body, and the physics lesson at every corner. More than likely, you'll step out wondering why such an effortlessly quick and surprisingly compact car feels so reluctant to go around corners. Welcome to the motorised conundrum that is the 911, the reason it has been such a compelling driver's car for so long. Like red wine, jazz music and smoked salmon, the 911's dynamics are an acquired taste. You won't appreciate how effective they can be or feel you're exploiting them until you've driven a 911 a few times, but once you've tuned in, you won't be able to stay away.

Yet if it is such an ultimately rewarding and beguiling layout, why have so few other sports car makers chosen to use it? Perhaps because the appeal of the Porsche isn't solely dynamic; it is also remarkably compact, famously reliable, surprisingly efficient and has great integrity. And, crucially, it's wonderfully tactile – its steering, pedals and gearshift have a consistent, engineered feel and weighting. It's a quality thing.

Mind, you can't wonder at the reluctance of other sports car makers to take on the 911 – every car that Porsche itself has designed since has been either mid- or front-engined. And, so far, the 911

has out-lived them all, relegating the 914, 924, 928, 944 and 968 to bit parts in the Porsche story.

The 911 shows no signs of relinquishing its position as top Porsche, either, even though it's now being pushed hard by the excellent mid-engined Boxster. The Boxster has been around for almost six years, yet it hasn't been able to prevent the 911 from driving off with our Car of the Year title no fewer than three times, the accolade going home with the standard 996 911, then the GT3 and last year the Turbo.

Now there's the GT2, which promises to combine the immediacy and involvement of the rear-drive GT3 with a bigger turbocharged thrill than the 4wd Turbo. Could that make it the best 911 ever?

Possibly, but without driving it back-to-back with the most impressive 911s that have gone before, how could we be sure? We couldn't, so we argued a bit and eventually agreed on nine must-have 911s with as strong a claim to the title of 'Best 911 Ever' as the GT2. Then we arranged for them all to be in North Yorkshire for a couple of days.

And here they are, brightening up a drizzle-soaked moorside, and suddenly it doesn't seem like such a simple idea. Ranged before us is a nape-tingling, stomach-flipping, insurance company-worrying array of 911s spanning almost 30 years, from 1972 to 2001. Chronologically they are: 2.7 RS, 3.0 RS, 959, 3.2 CS, 964 RS, 993 RS and GT2, and 996 GT3, Turbo and GT2. They are what we regard as the most entertaining, most engaging, most cohesive, most rewarding, most competent, most attractive, most thrilling and most desirable roadgoing 911s that Porsche has ever made. Where on earth do you start?

At the beginning seems most obvious, with the 2.7 RS.

➜

HARDCORE HERITAGE

■ 1973 Carrera RS

There were driver's 911s before this, but the unmistakable duck-tailed 2.7 is where the 911 legend really began. Developed by Porsche as a good basis for racing, the RS was endowed with terrific performance thanks to its newly enlarged 2687cc flat-six engine, which developed a healthy 210bhp at 6300rpm. Porsche needed to sell 500 for homologation purposes, but the 2.7 RS proved so popular that a total of 1590 were eventually produced, of which 55 were pure-bred RSR racers, 1308 were the more luxurious RS Touring, and just 227 were RS Lightweights. Tipping the scales at 975kg, the RS Lightweight was 100kg lighter than the Touring and could hit 60mph in 5.6sec and run on to 150mph. No wonder it is still rated by many as the ultimate 911. Best of all, an RS Touring can be yours for a little over £30,000. Tempting, isn't it?

■ 1995 993 Carrera RS

Like its illustrious ancestor, the 993 RS has a passionate following amongst 911 connoisseurs. The last air-cooled 911 to wear the RS badge, its 3.8-litre engine, with Porsche's Varioram induction system, produced a scintillating 300bhp, which it fired through the rear wheels via a six-speed gearbox. Built using the time-honoured RS recipe of thinner glass and body panels, the 993 RS also jettisoned interior luxuries in pursuit of lightness. As a result it was an impressive 100kg lighter than the cooking Carrera model, which, combined with lowered and stiffened suspension made it one of the sweetest-handling 911s ever. With just 47 of the 1123 production run coming in right-hand drive, the 993RS remains one of the most sought-after Porsches. Which means you're unlikely to see any change from £50K if you want to buy a good one.

FORGOTTEN HEROES

■ 1974 Carrera RS 3.0

Built in the wake of the 2.7 RS, the bigger-engined, broader-bodied RS 3.0 is one of the lesser-known race-bred 911s. Based on the new-for-'74 G-series 911, the RS 3.0 was the first 911 to wear the infamous 'whale tail' and engorged rear wheelarches that would later become synonymous with the Turbo. The engine was stretched to 2994cc, power increased to 230bhp, though it was effectively no quicker than the 2.7 (0-60 in 5.7sec and a top speed of 148mph) thanks in part to the increased drag generated by those broad hips and that wing. It was also heavier – though by no means heavy – tipping the scales at 900kg. The RS 3.0's lack of notoriety can partly be attributed to its extreme rarity. Just 111 were built: 54 road cars, 42 RSR competition versions and 15 special IROC versions for an American race series.

■ 1990 964 Carrera RS

Perhaps the most aggressively focussed RS of all, the 964 RS was built to satisfy both Porsche's motorsport needs and the buying public's desire for a pure-bred, hard-edged, driver's 911 after the introduction of the softer, all-weather Carrera 4 a year or so earlier. Pared down to 1229kg and with a modest power hike from the standard Carrera's 250bhp to 260bhp, the result was a 911 that could dash to 60mph in just over 5sec and comfortably breach 160mph. With its uncompromising suspension, it could also cope with the demands of circuit driving better than any previous road-going 911, though this overtly sporting character also drew criticism from the motoring press at the time. Recently available from as little as £20,000, values are now recovering, with the best cars today fetching nearly £30,000.

Engine: Flat-6, 2687cc, 12v, air cooled
Max power: 210bhp @ 6300rpm
Max torque: 188 @ 5100rpm
Kerb weight: 975kg
Power/weight: 219bhp/ton 0-60mph: 5.6sec
Top speed: 150mph Number built: 1590

Engine: Flat-6, 3746cc, 12v, air-cooled
Max power: 300bhp @ 6500rpm
Max torque: 262lb ft @ 5400rpm
Kerb weight: 1279kg
Power/weight: 238bhp/ton 0-60mph: 5.1sec
Top speed: 172mph Number built: 1123

Engine: Flat-6, 2994cc, 12v, air-cooled
Max power: 230hp @ 6200rpm
Max torque: 204lb ft @ 5000rpm
Kerb weight: 900kg
Power/weight: 259bhp/ton 0-60mph: 5.5
Top speed: 148mph Number built: 111

Engine: Flat-6, 3600cc, 12v, air-cooled
Max power: 260bhp @ 6100rpm
Max torque: 227lb ft @ 4800rpm
Kerb weight: 1229kg
Power/weight: 215bhp/ton 0-60mph 5.3sec
Top speed: 162mph Number built: 2364

THE APPLIANCE OF SCIENCE

2000 996 Turbo

Evo's reigning Car of the Year, the 996 Turbo still shocks with its ability to deliver effortless, enormous speed on any road and in any weather. Like the 959 before it, the Turbo's brief is to flatter rather than challenge its driver. Using the 911's inherent traction advantage and capitalising on it with all-wheel drive and a sophisticated stability control system, the 996 Turbo is quite simply the most exploitable supercar in the world. Heavier as a result of all-wheel drive and increased creature comforts, but more powerful thanks to its twin-turbocharged, 3.6-litre, 420bhp engine, the Turbo may lack a little of the purity and immediacy of its race-bred stablemates but broadens the range of conditions where a 911 can excel. Anyone who has felt its intoxicating accelerative squeeze and sheer ground-covering ability will vouch for that.

1986 959

Though originally conceived as a Group B racer, the 959's greatness is rooted not in motorsport glory but its advanced engineering. Boasting every technical innovation Porsche engineers could contain within its 911-derived bodyshell, the 959 was a technical tour de force. All-wheel drive with active torque split, driver selectable traction programs, electronically adjustable ride height and damper stiffness, water-cooled cylinder heads, multi-stage turbocharging, anti-lock brakes, advanced 'zero-lift' aerodynamics and composite bodywork. The 959 had all this and more. In fact if Porsche had charged customers what the car actually cost to produce, the asking price would have doubled. The world had never seen anything like it, nor would it again for more than two decades, until the introduction of the 996 Turbo.

RACERS AT HEART

1999 996 GT3

Not quite an 'RS', the GT3 nevertheless formed the basis for one of Porsche's most successful and prolific GT race cars. Built in limited numbers (just 50 rhd cars came to the UK), the GT3 shunned weight saving measures (it was actually heavier than the Carrera) in favour of more power and sharper dynamics. But the GT3's route to enhanced performance was no less effective. Using a dry-sumped, 360bhp, normally-aspirated development of the Le Mans-winning GT1 motor, the GT3's rev-hungry delivery brought a new dimension to the modern 911 experience. Bigger brakes and significantly lowered and stiffened suspension restored the keenness to the 996's more mellow edge, while the purity and lightness of rear-wheel drive endowed the GT3 with a 996 Turbo rivalling power-to-weight ratio. Undoubtedly one of the very best 911s.

1987 Carrera Club Sport

Based on the 3.2-litre Carrera, the Club Sport was, as its name suggested, built as a cost-effective club-level race car. Built without sound deadening, underseal or body cavity treatment, the CS was usefully lighter than the Carrera despite lacking RS-style thin-gauge glass and bodywork. It also had a keener 231bhp engine, thanks to a raised 6840rpm rev limit. Comparatively few CS models were built; Porsche buyers seemed more preoccupied with vulgar Turbo Cabrios, and it was an otherwise barren era for genuine Porsche driver's cars. Indeed, the CS was Porsche's first normally aspirated road-racer since the RS 3.0 of 1974. Denied the cachet of an RS tag, the Club Sport was understated proof that Porsche hadn't lost its touch where raw-edged, race-honed dynamics were concerned. A car shot through with essence of 911.

Engine: Flat-6, 3600cc, water-cooled, biturbo	Engine: Flat-6, 2850cc, water-cooled, biturbo
Max power: 420bhp @ 6000rpm	Max power: 450bhp @ 6500rpm
Max torque: 413lb ft @ 4600rpm	Max torque: 368lb ft @ 5000rpm
Kerb weight: 1540kg	Kerb weight: 1451kg
Power/weight: 272bhp/ton 0-60mph: 4.1sec	Power/weight: 315bhp/ton 0-60mph: 3.7sec
Top speed: 189mph Number built:	Top speed: 197mph Number built: 283

Engine: Flat-6, 3600cc, 24v, water-cooled	Engine: Flat-6, 3164cc, 12v, air-cooled
Max power: 360bhp @ 7200rpm	Max power: 231bhp @ 5900rpm
Max torque: 273lb ft @ 5000rpm	Max torque: 210lb ft @ 4800rpm
Kerb weight: 1350kg	Kerb weight: 1164kg
Power-to-weight: 271bhp 0-60mph: 4.5sec	Power/weight: 202bhp/ton 0-60mph: 4.9sec
Top speed: 187mph Number built: 1450	Top speed: 153mph Number built: 340

A RACE APART

1994 993 GT2

Combining the delicacy and lightness of the 993 RS with 430 explosive, twin-turbo'd horsepower, the 993 GT2 was designed with two things in mind: racing and winning. A fearsome-looking machine, complete with riveted-on wheelarch extensions, a high-rise rear wing with hungry air-intakes and a tarmac-skimming ride-height, the GT2 was the four-wheeled equivalent of fusing Prince Naseem's build with Lennox Lewis's punch, the most uncompromising 911 ever to go into production. Though an intimidating prospect on the road, those lucky enough to experience it were immediately surprised by its relatively docile dynamics, which retained many of the 993 RS's qualities. Costing well over £100,000 when new, the 993 GT2 was the most expensive, most exotic, most extreme 911 this side of the £600,000 911 GT1.

2001 996 GT2

The fastest 911 ever (excluding the 959). Quite an accolade, and one that rests firmly on the 996 GT2's broad shoulders. A combination of the GT3's back-to-basics drivetrain and the immense power of a beefed-up 996 Turbo engine, the 996 GT2 is the epitome of Porsche's new-school approach to building the ultimate driver's 911. With nothing but a limited-slip diff to contain the 455bhp passing through the rear wheels, the GT2 is a GT3 locked in hyper-drive. Clever aerodynamics rob its form of simple, unsullied beauty, and a lack of motorsport intent ensures it will never bask in the reflected glory its name-sake enjoyed, but if you're passionate about 911s, the new GT2 commands your full and undivided attention. Does it possess the depth of ability and involvement to earn a place alongside the very best 911s? You're in the right place to find out.

Engine: Flat-6, 3600cc, air-cooled, biturbo
Max power: 430bhp @ 5750rpm
Max torque: 398lb ft @ 4500rpm
Kerb weight: 1290kg
Power/weight: 339bhp/ton 0-60mph: 3.9sec
Top speed: 183mph Number built: 237

Engine: Flat-6, 3600cc, water-cooled, biturbo
Max power: 455bhp @ 5700rpm
Max torque: 457lb ft @ 3500-4500rpm
Kerb weight: 1440kg
Power/weight: 320bhp/ton 0-60mph: 4.0sec
Top speed: 196mph Number built:

Having shared the drive north with co-editor Meaden in the new GT2, I'm intrigued and a little apprehensive at the contrast that awaits in the shape of the original Carrera RS. But it quickly becomes apparent that this legendary 911 doesn't need the support of historical perspective to impress.

Unadorned by extravagant spoilers and wheelarch flares, its flanks underscored by the blood red 'Carrera' script, the RS looks incredibly small and narrow. It's hard to believe that this bodyshell is essentially the same as that of every other 911 here bar the three current-generation 996s – even the 959 was crafted around it.

Like most of us here, I've driven many 911s but never a 2.7 RS. As I slip behind the wheel I know I shouldn't be surprised at the familiarity of my surroundings, but I am. It's a weird kind of déjà vu, like watching the *Star Wars* movies and seeing the prequel long after you've enjoyed the exciting developments that follow. The view of the long, headlamp-capped front wings through the RS's upright screen is reassuringly distinctive, as is the churning rumble of the flat-six idling away behind.

There are plenty of features that date the RS – the liquorice-thin steering wheel rim, the long, bent-wand gear lever, and the shapeless-looking, short-backed 'bucket' seats – but in less than a mile the RS has established its credentials. Those seats prove surprisingly comfortable and supportive, the gearshift is long-winded but marvellously tactile and accurate, and there's no shortage of dynamic feedback. That spindly wheel rim tells you precisely what the front tyres are up to and through the driver's seat you can feel exactly what's happening at the rear.

For this I am grateful. There isn't such a thing as an 'ordinary' 2.7 RS but this one has a more illustrious provenance than any other: it was a highly successful racing car, campaigned by AFN, before it was bought by 911 collector Lord Mexborough in the mid-'80s. On these seriously puddled roads the RS is frantically, alarmingly alive, deflected by unavoidable pools of standing water but delicately responsive when they can be avoided. And when I eventually get to press its organ-pedal throttle to the floor… *Jeez!* does it fly. This 1973 911 is in rude health, and no mistake.

A fill-up (laying at least 40kg more over its front wheels) makes it even better, though it's already clear that Lord Mexborough keeps this RS in tip-top condition; it feels so together, so solid and free of creaks and rattles, and it's to the original spec, apart from a set of Pirelli P-Zeros which undoubtedly improve its grip enormously.

Co-ed Meaden, another 2.7 RS virgin, is as surprised by its performance as I am. 'Really punchy acceleration, made all the more memorable by instant throttle response and that terrific, dry, rasping engine note,' he enthuses. It's clear that the oldest car here has served notice on every other 911 that would claim to be the best ever.

Meaden again, after a run in the dry: 'The whole car feels so delicate, so deft, you hardly need to make any steering input to get the nose turned in. It's almost as though you *think* it into the apex.' Contributor Roger Green is just as amazed: 'It's so pure; every input provokes an immediate response and it's hugely satisfying. Only the brakes betray it's age but once you've acclimatised to them, you really start to crack on. What must it have been like on the roads in the early '70s?' Indeed. ➲

Where the 911 legend really began: the original, scintillating Carrera RS. It was also the first 911 with different size tyres front and rear – in fact the rear 215s were the widest rubber available at the time (1973)

'You hardly need to make any steering input to get the nose turned in. It's almost as though you think it into the apex'

'The 3.0 RS looks like it has driven straight out of an early '70s Steve McQueen film'

he next evolution of the 911 wasn't long coming. To stay ahead of its on-track rivals, the RS had to evolve, and so in 1974 Porsche unleashed its successor, the 3.0 RS.

Beyond the obvious up-sizing of the engine (which took power up from 210 to 230bhp and improved low-rev urge), the new RS sported body-building, attention-grabbing additions: flared wheelarches under which sheltered fatter rims and tyres, a distinctive chin spoiler with a hungrier, square air intake, and the very first 'whale-tail' spoiler.

While the 2.7 is almost timeless, the blue and gold liveried 3.0 RS is clearly a product of the early '70s. 'It looks like it has driven straight out of a Steve McQueen film,' comments Green. Despite the 3.0's rarity, its owner, Lord Mexborough, doesn't feel compelled to keep it in as fine fettle as his 2.7, which is rather telling.

'You know this is going to be a less delicate car to drive,' says Meaden, though he adds that it does feel more modern. 'You sit lower, the steering is heavier, the brakes bite more strongly and you have to adjust your driving style less to cope with it, making it an easier car to drive hard.' That was surely the conclusion of those that raced it, too, yet in road car terms the gain in grip and security is offset by a loss of delicacy and feedback. Although we're reluctant to judge it definitively given that this car isn't on modern tyres like the 2.7, it seems that evolution has sold the road driver a little short.

Even Meaden, keen to see the 3.0 RS in its best light, concludes that it is: 'Progress of sorts, but already that 2.7 magic was being diluted.'

Left: wider arches, fatter tyres, bigger air intakes – 3.0 RS has lost some of the visual delicacy of the 2.7, and that's reflected in the driving. Feels quite a bit more modern, though

t's a big jump to our next contender, the 959, and we fully accept that its place in this chronology of 911s is rather dubious. We include it not so much for its advancement of the 911 line back in '86 but as a presage of things to come. At the time, the roadgoing 911 Turbo was not long established and was a recalcitrant beast, a fast but blunt instrument. The 959 indicated how it might evolve, with two turbos instead of one and four-wheel drive instead of rear drive.

The 959 was engineered with a Germanic zeal, resulting in a 2.9-litre 24-valve flat-six producing 450bhp, a 4wd system with selectable dry, wet and snow settings (a feature that's a novelty even now on the Mitsubishi Evo VII), and a much wider chassis clothed in that distinctive, free-flowing bodywork.

I'm in the 2.7 RS when the 959's wide, pebble-smooth nose looms large in the rear-view mirror and it really does seem like I'm about to be overtaken by the 911 of the future. Green emerges with a wry smile; he's been waiting to drive a 959 since he had its poster on his

bedroom wall as a kid. So was it worth the wait? 'I feel privileged,' he says, but he's realistic: 'It's not the perfect driver's tool: the steering lacks the clarity and feel of the best here and it's as if you're expected to sit back and marvel at the brilliance of the Porsche engineers.'

The 959 isn't simply unlike any other 911; it's unlike any other car you'll ever drive. It will cover ground at remarkable speed – as fast as the current Turbo, we discovered – but it's a wild ride over these moorland roads. Pushed hard, body control is spongy, and grip and feedback ➔

Above: 959 has more switches, gauges and warning lights than any other 911, as befits its complex mechanicals. Purple/grey trim is probably an acquired taste

Unexpectedly, the 996 Turbo, which captured our Car of the Year title 12 months after the GT3, gets a decidedly lukewarm reception. It might be considerably more potent, but right from the off it quite clearly lacks the feel that marks out the truly great 911s – the standard is that high.

For me, its chances are blown within a mile of it taking on the same road as the GT3. A very light clutch pedal ruins the consistency of its controls, the suspension feels like it's running positive camber so the tyres don't feel like they're biting, and the sound of that 420bhp, turbocharged engine is uninspiring. Plant your right foot and the Turbo shifts all right, but the sound is so muted, just a windy roar, and with so little encouragement from the chassis how can you exploit its 4wd?

'The contrast between the Turbo and GT3 is stark,' agrees Meaden. 'Its steering feels treacly, its 4wd chassis cumbersome after the instinctive rear-drive GT3. It's stupidly rapid even at seven-tenths but it's almost as though Porsche decided that the driver was always going to be the weakest link and so removed them from the equation.' Hayman isn't enamoured, either.

'It may have won eCOTY, but in this company it has returned to being the effective but dull car it was on the big supercar test (**evo** 22). Fast and very capable no matter who's behind the wheel, but unrewarding.' Nuff said.

Above: current Turbo is comfiest, most refined and easiest to drive quickly of all the 911s. It's also one of the least engaging

'The 996 Turbo is stupidly rapid even at seven-tenths, but it's almost as though the driver has been removed from the equation'

'Step on the gas and the new GT2 goes like few other cars this side of a McLaren F1'

996 GT2 is massively impressive in the metal, looking like a much meaner, slightly scary version of the Turbo, which is effectively what it is. And rear-wheel drive only of course, which helps focus the mind...

So, what about the 996 GT2, the car that promises to combine the best elements of GT3 and Turbo? It certainly looks the part with its aggressive stance, its wheels and tyres filling its arches almost as fully as the 964 RS's. It makes the GT3 look a bit undernourished, in fact.

I drove it straight after its daddy, the 993 GT2, and I reckon it's quicker. Partly this is because it has even less turbo lag, though even deep into the full-on, maximum boost rush, there's nothing in it. Step on the gas and the new GT2 goes like few other cars this side of a McLaren F1. Porsche claims 0-62mph in 4.1sec and 196mph flat-out and the GT2 feels good for it. Think how little faster the 959 goes and then consider the GT2's £109,800 price tag.

The new GT2 is a hardcore 911 all right, but I don't think it delivers everything it promises. You can't argue with its staggering performance but its chassis isn't as decisive, as keen and communicative as it ought to be. Sure, it states its intention with its lack of traction control (don't bother searching its dashboard for the PSM stability control button) but it ought to arm you with copious, detailed feedback so that you can tell when you're getting close to the edge. Sadly it doesn't.

It'll go far faster than the legal limit in absolute security, but that's shallow entertainment, particularly in this company. The Porsche GB press office tells us that the suspension can be adjusted to neutralise the understeer but that alone wouldn't turn it into a faster GT3. The GT2 simply isn't as precise and rewarding a tool.

Everyone is gob-smacked by its pace but left a little cold. 'It feels a bit blunt in the steering department and there's a nasty, skittery feeling when you load up the front tyres which makes it an unnerving thing to push hard,' says Meaden, adding: 'It's almost as though the front tyres never warm up, and it's not much better at the rear – the tail seems to slip into a few degrees of oversteer without you knowing it.'

Green agrees. 'It's hard to predict what it's going to do. The more I drove the more I got to grips with it, but it never completely gelled.' Bovingdon was equally bemused. 'It's very unusual for a Porsche to feel so out of sorts. I can't remember the last time a new Porker opened itself up to such criticism in the handling department. Disappointing.'

The only dissenting voice is Hayman's. 'After sitting alongside Meaden and experiencing its tendency to snap from understeer into oversteer I was, to say the least, a little wary. I suppose I wanted and expected a faster GT3, which it isn't. You have to bully it or be bullied. I did gain confidence and then it becomes an absolute joy to push, as long as the road is dry. But respect is due at all times.' ➔

Above: GT2 in Club Sport spec comes with winged Recaro seats and a beefy roll-cage – just the thing for track days

So, what is the 'Greatest 911 Ever'? Not the new GT2, that's for sure. In fact, not any turbocharged 911, though John Hayman has been blown away by the earlier 993 GT2 and wants to elope with it when nobody's looking. Meaden has praise for the 993 GT2, too: 'The greatest turbocharged 911,' he declares, 'but not the greatest 911.'

Overall, it's the normally aspirated cars that have monopolised our enthusiasm, though perhaps that shouldn't be a surprise. Enjoying the 911's tail-heavy layout, making it work for you and reaping its unique rewards – this is at the very heart of the 911 experience, and best achieved with a finely responsive engine. And so on our short list we have the 2.7 RS, Club Sport, 964 RS and 996 GT3.

What this absorbing comparison also reveals is that the formula that created the original, compelling 911, the 2.7 RS, has been pretty much emulated by its successors. But which is the one? It's not easy because, as Meaden says, picking the best is like trying to decide between great racing drivers from different eras; the 2.7 RS is Fangio, the GT3 Schumacher, and there's Jim Clark and Senna in there, too. They're all brilliant and you can construct valid arguments for each of them.

So let's get personal. To my mind, the best 911 ever should be the model that is most 911-like, which makes mine a short list of two – 2.7 RS and Club Sport. And much as I love the 2.7, the CS has its looks, a more engaging and vocal engine, a more tactile gearshift and better brakes. I could own it and not hanker after any other.

Meaden is also a fan of both. 'No wonder the 2.7 is regarded as the source of the 911 legend,' he says. 'It has the purest shape, the best balance of power, weight and grip and delivers the most involving, absorbing driving experience of the lot. You could drive this car all your life and still learn something new from it. Glorious.'

He describes the Club Sport as 'probably the most involving after the 2.7' and marvels that it's the most affordable car here, but there's a third car fighting for his affections. It's not the GT3, though we're agreed this is the greatest of the current-generation cars. No, Dickie's smitten with the 964 RS. 'Of the modern era cars, this is the one I really lust after,' he says. After a heated debate with himself, the like of which I've only ever seen on *Who wants to be a millionaire?*, he plumps for… the 2.7 RS.

He's in good company. Lord Mexborough, a dedicated driver and collector of Ferraris and Porsches, holds the 2.7 in the highest regard: 'It's a fine driver's car, the finest, I think.' Green is in love, too, musing: 'If you had one you'd never sell it. It's a true classic in every sense.' Ah, but is it his definitive choice, I wonder? 'The 964 RS comes very close to winning for me; it's a perfect bridge between the old and new, it retains the scale and nimbleness of the early cars whilst including a few modern comforts such as decent brakes. But even so, some of that original purity has gone, it doesn't quite have the magic of 2.7 RS and, as usual, my heart rules my head.'

Bovingdon, who was just a twinkle in his father's trousers when the 2.7 RS was launched, is amazed. 'How good is this? Almost 30 years old but still bloody brilliant.' His favourite, then? 'The stupid grin on everyone who drove it tells you all you need to know. Others cover ground more quickly but none delivers the undiluted thrills that this does. Put simply, it's the most engaging car I've ever driven.'

So, there you have it. The consensus after two days' driving is that the greatest is the 2.7 RS, which is also the oldest of our group. I can't help feeling that there's a message here for Porsche, if it's interested. The new GT2 is a sensational car but the most impressive of the recent 911s is the GT3. 'By far the best 996 generation car,' says Meaden. 'Maybe one day I will find something I do not like about this car,' adds Hayman.

And it wouldn't have taken much to put the GT3 into close-quarters contention with the 2.7 RS, either – maybe a few less creature comforts, some thinner glass, a few lightweight panels…

In short, what we'd really like is a 996 RS. Come on Porsche, we know you can do it.

Many, many thanks to those without whom this feature would not have been possible: Lord Mexborough, Richard Green, John Probert, Adrian Rowlands, Steve Harding-Roberts, Jim Palmer, Steve Walker, and the Porsche Club GB (tel 01608 652911, fax 01608 652944, e-mail: hqpcgb@btinternet.com or website: porscheclubgb.com).

'No wonder the 2.7 is regarded as the source of the 911 legend'

EXCESS ALL AREAS

Though the idea of modifying a 911 is sacrilege to some, a number of German tuning specialists have successfully enhanced the performance of Porsche's legendary supercar. Ruf, TechArt and Gemballa have all put their own spin on the 911, and though the results are sometimes in rather poor taste, certain cars have been devastatingly effective.

One of the most famous tuned 911s was Ruf's CTR. With a 463bhp turbocharged motor slotted into the narrow 3.2 Carrera bodyshell, the CTR was a genuine 200mph car – and handled too. If you've seen the infamous Faszination video, in which test driver Stefan Roser drives Ruf's heroic demo CTR, Yellowbird, around the Nürburgring in awesomely sideways style, you'll know the fastest 911s don't necessarily come straight from Stuttgart.

More recent proof can be found in the form of TechArt's 600bhp GT Street, based on the 996 Turbo, which has just lowered the outright road car lap record of the Nürburgring to a barely believable 7min 43.4sec. Driven by an independent test driver, German motoring magazine Sport Auto's editor Horst von Saurma, it destroyed the new GT2's recent production car record of 7min 49sec set in the hands of the vastly experienced Walter Röhrl.

Ruf's legendary CTR (below) and TechArt's awesome GT Street (right), in 2001 holder of the road car lap record at the Nürburgring

THE ONES THAT GOT AWAY

There are a number of 'ultimate' 911s that we might have included in this test, starting with the 911 GT1. Although we did track down one example in the UK, sadly the owner wasn't able to supply the car. Though the prospect of threading half a million quids' worth of thinly disguised Le Mans racer across the north Yorks moors would have had our insurers taking up permanent residence in the executive toilets, it would have been an awe-inspiring, if ultimately terrifying experience. And since it is so far removed from roadgoing reality, not a very illuminating one.

Any of the pure race RSR models (or indeed the super lightweight late-'60s 911R) would also have been fantastic, but in the end we decided their no-compromise characters and extreme rarity precluded them.

Then there were the two incarnations of the little-known Turbo S model. Both the two-wheel-drive, 380bhp, single-turbo car, and the later all-wheel drive, 430bhp, twin-turbo version were fabulous, combining non-turbo deftness with explosive turbocharged power, but our findings suggest they would have struggled to beat the best of the non-turbo 911s.

We could have made a case for several of the more humble Carrera models (and indeed the original 964 model Carrera 4) but simple logistics meant we had to draw a line. Deciding which cars to include was the easy bit. Deciding which to leave out was tougher.

The GT1 that got away: ultra-rare million-dollar roadgoing racer. Below: Turbo S would have been on the pace

1989 saw the launch of a new 911, known as the 964. It appeared first in 4wd Carrera 4 form (this page), quickly followed by 2wd Carrera 2 which then spawned the stripped-out 964RS (right). The 964 is bursting with 911 character – but there are also plenty of potential pitfalls for the unwary buyer, which is where this guide comes in

PORSCHE
964 CARRERA & RS

The 964 version of the 911 looks hugely tempting – especially the lightweight RS version – but you need to know your stuff

Words: Jethro Bovingdon and Roger Green **Pictures:** Andy Morgan

For many, the 964 was the last of the classic 911s. Its shape and size had changed little from the early '70s and its diminutive stature and relative technical simplicity gave it a delicious nimbleness and a rawness of character that faded in subsequent models. Of course there will always be those who just don't get 911s, citing the rear engine as an inherent flaw rather than a magic ingredient. But one short drive is all it takes for a 964 to cast its spell. This 911 feels special immediately, from the sonorous flat-six yowl to the gently bobbing nose and beautiful steering, and after the briefest of drives you'll want one. It's that sort of car.

The good news is that you might just be able to afford one. While the 993 levels out at around £22K,

the older, classic-shaped 964 is tantalisingly cheap. If you're prepared to sit on the left hand side of the car you could be snugly ensconced in a 964 for as little as £12,000 and you won't need much more than £15,000 for a UK-spec car. It seems a small price to pay to own a legend.

If you are tempted by a 964 you'll be spoiled for choice. There is always a massive selection for sale and Porsche's diverse model range means there's a 964 for everybody. If you're worried about that pendulous rear-mounted engine, then a 4wd Carrera 4 might ease you're nerves. Whether you opt for rear or four-wheel drive there is the choice of coupe, Targa or Convertible, and if you go for a C2 you can even get an auto! (Not that we'd recommend it.)

For the ultimate expression of 911 thrills the 964 also has a stripped-out contender. The lightweight

964RS is about as pure a 911 as you'll find from any era. With no sound-deadening, little interior trim and a punishing ride, it's not your everyday usable supercar. But if you want an occasional toy for trackdays and the odd early-morning blast the 964RS is an awesome tool. Criticised at launch it has matured in to one of the most sought after Porsches amongst those in the know and prices have been rising dramatically over the last few years as this most potent of 964s has risen to something approaching iconic status. Get one quick, before the prices go up any further.

Be it Carrera 2, 4 or RS you'll be getting a landmark Porsche, but you need to be very careful during the buying process or things could get very expensive. The 964 was the first attempt at a truly modern 911 and it suffers from more problems than just about ➡

C4 interior (above) is absolutely classic 911 – no frills, solid build quality, scattered switchgear and floor-hinged pedals

WHAT THEY SAID AT THE TIME

'Where the old 911 dared you to tame it, the Carrera 2 begs you to enjoy it. There's no loss of the fun factor, because the steering is as involving as ever, the turn-in as positive and the engine as inspiring. Indeed, the fun factor goes up because you can explore the limits without biting your lip and being brave' - **Performance Car**

'There's no other production car we've driven able to match the pulverising response of the RS Carrera... it goes and stops better than almost anything else you can buy' - **Autocar**

Specification

Porsche 964 Carrera 2

Layout	Longitudinal rear engine, rear-wheel drive
Engine	6 cylinders horizontally opposed, 3600cc
Max power	250bhp @ 6100rpm
Max torque	228lb ft @ 4800rpm
Gearbox	Five-speed manual/Four speed auto
Suspension	Front: MacPherson struts, lower wishbones coil springs, telescopic dampers, arb
	Rear: Semi-trailing arms, coils, t'scopic dampers, arb
Steering	Rack and pinion, PAS, 2.9 turns lock to lock
Brakes	Front: 298mm vented discs
	Rear: 299mm solid discs
Wheels	6 x 16in front, 8 x 17in rear, alloy
Tyres	205/55 ZR 16 front, 225/50 ZR 17 rear
Power to weight	188bhp per ton
0-60mph	5.5 seconds (claimed)
Max speed	162mph (claimed)

any other model. Having said that, if you find a good 964 it will provide you with endless fun. Porsche managed to retain the essential 911 character whilst massively improving refinement and making the wayward rear much less of an issue. The 964 can still bite, any 911 can, but it gives you a sporting chance should you provoke a slide. Compact, fast and rewarding, the 964 is everything a 911 should be. And isn't there a saying that everyone should own a Porsche once in their life? Well, there is now.

Evolution

The 964 first appeared in 1989 in Carrera 4 guise. It was the first large volume Porsche to feature 4wd and was welcomed with open arms by the motoring press. The 959, a masterful technical showcase, had wowed everybody that had driven it and the new 964 Carrera 4 was billed as a 959 for the common man (relatively speaking, of course).

It replaced the 3.2 model and Porsche claimed that the Carrera 4 was 85 per cent new. Quite apart from the 4wd system, the 964 was improved in every area. The engine grew to 3.6 litres thanks to an increase in bore and stroke to 100mm x 76.4mm (from 95mm x 74.4mm) and new cylinder heads, pistons, conrods and twin-plugs per cylinder helped to liberate plenty of horses. Power was up to 250bhp at 6100rpm while torque was a strong 228lb ft at 4800rpm. This translated to a 0-60mph time of just over five seconds and a claimed maximum speed of 162mph (exactly the same as the contemporary 300bhp Turbo) – the latter due to massively improved aerodynamics (a Cd figure of .32, down from .395)

The 4wd system itself wasn't that of the 959, although it did share a number of features with the ultimate 911 derivative. Porsche decided on a 31/69

split of power front to rear. However, as much as 100 per cent of power could be channelled to one axle or the other in slippery conditions. The practical implications of the 4wd system and the new semi-trailing-arm and coil spring suspension at the rear were increased security over previous 911s but also more obvious understeer during fast road driving. The Carrera 4 will still oversteer but it can feel a little unresponsive to those used to rear-wheel-drive 911s.

The Carrera 2 was introduced a year later in 1990 and the underlying worries about the Carrera 4's chassis were suddenly brought into sharp focus. The C2 had all the security you could ask for without the irksome understeer. The Carrera 4 is by no means a bad car but the new rear-drive 964 made it look a little unnecessary. At 1380kg, the C2 was 70kg lighter than the C4 and substantially quicker.

As with the C4, the C2 was also a much more sophisticated car than the outgoing 3.2-litre car. Power steering and ABS were now standard and there were a raft of improvements both internally and externally. The pop-up rear spoiler that raised automatically at 50mph was also shared with the C4. The Carrera 2 did have one option that the C4 didn't have and that was the Tiptronic four-speed automatic option. Porsche was the first to introduce the idea of an auto that could be controlled manually with just a flick of the lever. Performance suffered but the Tiptronic 'box was a popular option.

A model that couldn't have appealed to a more different audience was the 964RS. Introduced in '91, the RS ditched the C2's air-con, electric seats and windows, power steering, central locking and rear seats and in a further quest for lightness added thinner glass, an aluminium bonnet, composite Recaros, Turbo-spec front brakes, rear discs from the Carrera Cup racer and a set of 17in magnesium alloys. The body was seam-welded to improve structural rigidity, too.

The RS weighed in at 1230kg and with power up to 260bhp (thanks to different engine management) it absolutely flew. Faster in a straight line, better under braking and set up almost exclusively for track work it is, perhaps, the most focussed 911 ever. In all, 2364 RS models left the factory and only 47 were officially brought to the UK, so if you are after a hardcore 911 an imported RS may be the way to go. There was also a 'Touring' option, which put back many of the Carrera 2's luxury items but retained the more powerful engine. Very few RS Tourings were ordered (about 50 from the total production run). The RSR was an even more stripped-out version of the RS. Interior trim was ditched and a rollcage was standard factory fit. As trackday cars, the 964 RS and RSR are almost perfect.

Production of the 964 ended in December '93 and as well as the models outlined above there were a few other variants. The Speedster made its debut in '93 but very few made it to the UK. The ultimate RS – the RS 3.8 with 300bhp, 18-inch magnesium wheels and a big twin-blade spoiler – was also introduced in '93. Just 129 were built. But the most extreme 964 of all was the Carrera 4 Lightweight. Intended purely for racing, this competition-focused 4wd 964 weighed only 1100kg thanks to aluminium panels, plexiglass side windows and a fibreglass engine cover. It used the RS engine with some modifications to produce 300bhp. Around 20 were built in left-hand-drive only and very rarely come up for sale.

'I bought one'

Andy Caisey

'As I commute into London by train I wanted a car to have fun in at the weekend. I was brought up on GTIs and had done the Impreza thing, now I wanted a car with character and soul. I had always admired the whole 911 history and ethos, so the search began. First I had to decide which version of 911. I didn't want to spend 996 money (plus they are water-cooled, which to me just isn't right). I thought the 993 had lost some of the raw 911 appeal and starting looking for a 964. I decided on a Carrera 4 for those wet winter nights, just to be safe.

'I started looking for cars at dealers and found a few that were nice but not what I was looking for. There was a number of ropey cars that had seen better days but were still top money. My next port of call was titanic.co.uk/porsche which runs the 964 register via email. I joined this to ask the members for advice, which I got by the bucketful. The best thing was that no question was too silly as they had

all been through the same experience. Then one of the members emailed to say that he was selling his Carrera 4. I visited him, the car had full history, was below 50,000 miles and the deal was done. The thing I realised was that knowing the owner and history was more important than the mileage.

'What I enjoy about the car is the cracking pace and the noise it makes. The South East is roundabout infested and the Carrera 4 makes every one a second-gear challenge to enjoy. Best of all, though, is that it can be used every day if you want, and I can get my wife and my young boy in the car and have enough room for luggage for a holiday break.

'So, what next? I think I need to build another garage to get another 964 purely for track use!'

Graham Tricker

'Having reached 43, I thought it was about time that I bought myself a proper sports car before I got too old to actually drive it! I've done quite a lot of motorsport and decided I wanted something with real track breeding but also the ability to cut it on the road. An Ultima was just a bit too impractical.

'A friend, Adrian Palmer, suggested I try a 964RS and arranged for me to have a ride in one around Bedford Autodrome. After a few fast laps I realised this was the car I was looking for. Adrian's associate Tom Schmitz of H&S Automobiles (a company that specialises in finding lightweight Porsches) started the hunt for a low-mileage RS soon after. It took seven months to track down a genuine RS with very low mileage but it was worth the wait. Tom found the car in Italy and promised me that it was perfect.

'I picked it up in Germany and wasn't disappointed. It had 6000 kilometres on the clock and looked brand new. Since then I've added 4000 kilometres and it has been a real privilege. As soon as you slide into those figure-hugging Recaros you know you're in for a wild ride and when the engine explodes into life you need to be ready to drive. The track-biased set-up means a very unforgiving ride on bumpy B-roads but the unfettered feedback through the unassisted steering is sublime and road driving is still huge fun.

'In terms of sheer performance the RS is simply staggering. The acceleration is fierce in virtually any gear and never seems to tail off, even well past 100. The RS is certainly an acquired taste but if you like your thrills served up raw, it's the ride of your life.'

'I decided on a Carrera 4 for those wet winter nights, just to be safe'

J713 WMO

Andy Caisey bought this Carrera 4 and hasn't looked back. Graham Tricker went for the RS, with slightly more power from the flat-six (above centre) and more Spartan cabin (above right)

Driving a 964RS today

Richard Meaden explains what makes the RS so special

Like many of you, I had my opinion of the 964-generation 911RS coloured by contemporary road test reports, which focussed on its unyielding ride. More race-car than road-car, it was deemed fatally flawed as a B-road machine and consequently failed to achieve the hero status bestowed upon the earlier 2.7RS and later 993RS.

That was in 1991, but fast-forward to today and the 'black sheep' of the 911 family is rapidly being reappraised. Light, aggressive and perfectly suited to the fast-evolving generation of trackday users, the 964RS is now regarded by many as one of the most exciting 911s of all.

It's not that the testers of the time were wrong – it was just about the most focussed, hardcore road car of its day rather that our tastes and expectations of what a fast road car should be have altered as the intensity of cars like Subarus and Mitsubishis has increased.

With 260bhp to hurl its 1229kg down the road, the 964RS is still a force to be reckoned with. It always feels fast and responsive, every squeeze of the throttle punching you forward with apparently equal vigour whether you're doing 50mph or 100mph. Dynamically it combines the deftness of a 2.7 with modern grip levels and braking ability. You can sense the engine hanging out in the breeze,

but the balance stays just the right side of edgy.

The suspension is hard, even by today's standards, but so long as you can put up with the kidney punches over bumpy roads the 964 is happy to soak up the punishment and rarely gets deflected. You can push hard but you need commitment and ability to remain on top of it. It's a raw thrill the like of which Porsche hasn't managed to replicate since. In the world of 911s, the 964RS is the real deal.

The 964RS (the pink car above, and below) feels quick even by current standards. The 964 Turbo (the blue car, above) was even quicker, but that's another story, another buying guide

'It combines the deftness of a 2.7 with modern grip levels and braking ability'

Richard Meaden loved the 964RS so much when he drove one for an **evo** feature that he eventually bought his own (below), and very fine it was too

Porsche 964 prices

■ £10,000 - £12,000

Left-hand-drive examples with high mileage fall into this price range. Ascertain the car's history carefully and walk away if it doesn't have a nicely stamped book and a fistful of bills. High mileage isn't always a problem (most 964s have racked up plenty of miles), but remember that these cars are up to 13 years old and will probably need some money spent on them. Paying a specialist to check the car over for you could save you a fortune in the long run – but be prepared for bills even if the car seems sound.

■ £13,000 - £16,000

The cheapest right-hand-drive models come in at about £15K and you'll find '92 and '93 lhd 964s at around this price, too. Targas are slightly more expensive than the equivalent coupe, but check for leaks and be prepared to put up with plenty of wind noise.

■ £18,000 - £21,000

The very best and lowest mileage 964s may command this sort of money but they aren't necessarily going to be any less prone to oil leaks, etc. Convertibles can also be had if you've got this much to spend.

■ Over £30,000

The soughtafter RS cars are getting more expensive by the year and you're unlikely to find one at much less than £30,000 . A right-hand-drive RS is even more expensive. Expect to pay £40,000 or more.

? Useful contacts

Autofarm (service and inspection) 01865 331234
Camtune (service) 08707 555911
Paragon (sales and service) 01825 830424
MCP Motorsport (sales – RS) 01263 822481
Porsche Club GB 01608 652911
964 Register 01608 652911

! Checkpoints

The 964 has a couple of serious flaws and you need to be vigilant to avoid some huge bills. Before you get to the mechanicals, check the VIN number, which is located on the left hand side of the front boot. The 10th digit reveals the year of manufacturer – not necessarily the same year the car was registered. '89 cars will have a 10th digit of K, '90 is L, '91 M, '92 N and '93 P. Carefully check the service history, then get the car on a ramp. The serious problems will be obvious underneath. Autofarm, a leading Porsche specialist, charge £150 + VAT to do an inspection on their premises. If you can't get the car to them, try some other specialists – but don't buy one of these cars blind. It could cost you thousands.

○ Engine

The single biggest problem with the 964 is oil leaks. There are two sources and both can cost a fortune to put right. One weakness is at the cylinder base. Instead of a gasket the 964 uses a machined metal to metal seal at the base of the cylinders and over time the part can distort and need replacing. Later cars (post '91) are less likely to be affected but any 964 can suffer. The engine is protected by an undertray – check to see if it is oily. Small leaks quickly become major and at its worst the rear of the car will be splattered with oil when the car is on the move. The fix requires rebuilding the top of the engine, and you have to take the engine out to do this. While it's out you'll probably want to change the piston rings and the valves and valve-guides. So a hefty bill of £2800 or so can easily swell to £4300.

The other source of leaks is the pipework that carries the oil from the oil-tank (located in a rear wheel arch) to the engine via a thermostat. The system is a mixture of rigid metal pipe and flexible pipe and where the two join corrosion is common. The pipes are clearly visible, once the engine's undertray is removed, near the back of the engine. If there is a leak the pipes need replacing. The parts will cost £400 + VAT but the work required to replace them is very time-consuming. The oil tank must be removed and when it is the other pipes around it snap, requiring even more work. A small leak can quickly escalate into a bill for £1000.

○ Transmission

The 964's gearbox is a robust unit but there are problems associated with the parts around it. The clutch isn't adjustable so if it bites very low then it's on the way out. The action should be smooth and not too weighty. If it feels notchy then it is likely that the needle roller-bearings on which the clutch fork pivots have dried out and need replacing. Again, parts aren't

massively expensive but replacing the clutch means taking out the engine and a bill of around £1000. If you can find a car with a new clutch you'll be saving a lot of money.

Other problems are with the dual-mass flywheel, designed to reduce noise in the cabin. One flywheel is bolted to the crankcase; another is located on the gearbox. Between the two is a thick grease that is supposed to act as a damper, reducing vibration and noise. There is a mechanism to stop the flywheels oscillating at different rates but this can break; you'll notice clonking at low revs if there's a problem. Later cars had a revised unit that is more reliable and many early cars have been converted.

○ Brakes

Porsche brakes are renowned for their power and the 964's are no exception. However, there is a common fault that needs to be looked for. The callipers themselves are made of alloy but the pads are fitted onto steel back plates. The alloy and steel react over time and begin to push apart – effectively pushing the pads closer to the discs. This leads to severe binding, which will eat pads and discs. Fixing the problem isn't easy and can cost £600 + VAT.

○ Suspension

You'll be relieved to hear there are no problems with the rear suspension. The front is a different story, though. The front aluminium lower wishbones pivot on rubber bushes. The front ones are prone to perishing and separating from their steel outer sleeve. On a test drive, cars with split bushes will feel very sloppy because the front wheels are not located effectively. Most cars will need new bushes unless they've been recently replaced.

The 964 is very sensitive to geometry settings and needs to be set-up by a specialist to Porsche factory settings to handle properly. Uneven tyre wear at the back indicates incorrect geometry settings.

Cliff
Two fabulous new street racers, Porsche 911 GT3 and Ferrari 360
Hanger

Stradale, meet on one of Europe's most challenging roads, the dizzying Stelvio Pass

Stelvio Pass in far north of Italy is famous for extreme altitude and plethora of hairpins (far right), although it's also blessed with sections of more open, flowing corners. It's a severe test of our pair of stripped-out road-racers

higher profile tyres, and when it moves around it is far more progressive and friendly. I'm sure that the Porsche has the greater lateral grip and, in the right hands, on a tighter track, might even post quicker lap times, but I couldn't help feeling that the McLaren driver would be having the more fun. You may think that I was more relaxed in the Mac because I know it better (although I hadn't driven this silver example before) but I don't think that was a major factor. I think that if you drive two cars back to back, you're going to feel the differences. And I did. I found the Carrera GT the easier road car and the McLaren the easier track car, the opposite of what I was expecting.

This was a great day. A fascinating duel between two fascinating cars and obviously the harshest comparative test to which the Carrera GT could be subjected. And yet it shone: it is a lovely car. But – and this I think is the essence of it – it

was designed to make money. Porsche lost a lot of money on its last super-duper car, the 959, and it was clearly determined not to make the same mistake this time. Hence the borrowed instrument binnacle, the endless airbags, stability electronics, PAS, etc, which may bring a 250kg weight penalty but also bring a wider acceptance (in the US, particularly) and justify a high target production of 1500 cars.

At a pretty reasonable price. In case you think that's the assertion of someone who's clearly lived on Planet Daft Car for too long, think on this. If the McLaren was made now, it would probably cost a million pounds. After reading what you've read, does £330,000 sound like too much for the Porsche?

The Carrera GT is one of the best sports cars ever made. But the McLaren is significantly faster and more special. Which is a result that should neither surprise nor offend anyone. ■

P O R S C H E
996

The sports car
you can use
every day without
questioning your
sanity. Here's
what to look for

Words: Roger Green **Pictures:** Andy Morgan

S632 UNE

www.porsche.co.uk/midsussex

You can safely say that the **evo** crew are big fans of the 911. Reading through past **evo** Car of the Year competitions it soon becomes apparent why. The 996 Carrera 2 won the inaugural crown in 1998 with its ability to be 'approachable and accessible like a sports car, but still with the ability to inspire awe like a supercar'. Which sums it up pretty neatly really. On paper it may have its heart in the wrong place, but on the road its purity of purpose, poise, finesse and honed athleticism allowed it to dominate a test that included the Ferrari F355 and the Elise 135.

A year later Porsche retained the crown, the GT3 smashing the hopes of twelve impressive contenders, and the 420bhp Turbo made it a hat-trick at the end of the millennium year. The 996 was in danger of making our biggest test of the year a forgone conclusion.

So they're good then. The best from the period in fact. And get this: you can pick up a very tidy example for less than £16,000. Early Carrera 2s with around 80,000 miles on the clock are in this price bracket. Buy wisely and reliability will be strong, running costs manageable, and depreciation virtually zero.

The C2 is just the starting point though. The complete 996 range requires further investigation as it includes the equally brilliant C4, the superb C4S, the potent Turbo and the electrifying GT3 – not to mention the convertibles, the Targa, the Turbo S and the mad, bad GT2. Right now all represent good value for money, making the 996 one of the most desirable second-hand buys around. ➡

996 CARRERA 2 ('98–'01 model years)

■ **Layout**	Rear engine, rear-wheel drive
■ **Engine**	3387cc, flat-six
■ **Power**	300bhp @ 6800rpm
■ **Torque**	258lb ft @ 4600rpm
■ **Suspension**	Front: MacPherson struts, lower wishbones, arb
	Rear: multi-link, arb
■ **Tyres**	225/40 ZR18 front, 265/35 ZR18 rear
■ **Power to weight**	231bhp/ton
■ **0-60mph**	4.6sec
■ **Top speed**	173mph
■ **Price when new**	£55,950

Flat-bottomed headlights mark this out as a pre-facelift 996 Carrera 2, meaning 300bhp from a 3387cc flat-six. Revised model, introduced late 2001, saw increase to 3.6 litres and 316bhp

Factory stickers (below centre) suggest originality. 996 interior ergonomics (right) a vast improvement over earlier 911s

Evolution

The 996 arrived in the autumn of 1997, costing £55,950. It was an impressive move forward from the 993, building on everything that had always been great about the 911. It was also the first water-cooled 911, meaning that the flat-six could use four valves per cylinder, power rising to 300bhp from the 3387cc unit.

The 996 was the first truly modern 911 – drive a 993 today and, by comparison, it will feel great but old, almost like a classic with its archaic switchgear and awkward ergonomics. The new car was more practical too, and while we don't

necessarily get excited by the fact that more bags could be squashed into the nose, the cabin was usefully roomier. The car's structure was also 45 per cent stiffer, yet despite all of this the 996 was 50kg lighter than the outgoing model. It was no surprise when sales took off rapidly, helped further by the introduction of the cabriolet in July '98.

In 1999 a side impact protection system was added, along with a new exhaust system. Cars so-equipped can be identified by their clear indicator lenses. The same year also saw the arrival of the Carrera 4 (fitted with Porsche's PSM stability control system) and the GT3. On

first acquaintance it can be hard to detect much of a difference between the C4 and the C2 as only five per cent of the drive is transferred to the front in normal driving conditions. However, up to 40 per cent can be transferred depending on a number of variables including rear wheel slip.

The 1999 eCoty winner was something special. The GT3 stripped the Carrera of all distractions, dropped the suspension by 30mm and upped power to 360bhp. Lighter, forged pistons, titanium con-rods and a 2mm longer stroke increased the swept volume to 3600cc. Unsurprisingly, the GT3 is one of the slowest depreciators of the lot and you'll need at least £35,000 to get into one. It's most definitely worth it though.

In 2000, PSM became available as an option on the C2 and further upgrades included a new engine management system and a drive-by-wire throttle (E-gas). The big news, however, was the introduction of the Turbo model. It may not have been quite as intimate as the C2, but it was a high-speed tour de force, able to rocket down any B-road you threw at it.

The big hitter, the GT2, landed in February 2001. Weighing 110kg less than the Turbo, it featured a 462bhp turbo engine, ceramic brakes, rock solid suspension and no PSM. And if the £110,000 price tag was a little steep, the wide-body C4S that arrived in September 2001 may

have been the answer. For a £2610 premium over the C4, it was fitted with the Turbo body, wider track, larger wheels and tyres, a lowered chassis, bigger brakes and sports seats. It was brilliant, incisive, dynamic and keyed to the road. Unsurprisingly it was an instant hit and residuals for the C4S are still very strong. Since 2001 a C4S will have lost £30,000 from new; a GT2 owner, however, would have seen over £70,000 disappear.

The most significant model upgrade arrived with the 2002 facelift, where headlight and bumper changes mark a number of under-the-skin revisions including a 316bhp 3.6-litre engine with Variocam Plus. Aerodynamics were subtly improved along with crash protection and rigidity, while inside there was a new steering wheel and a revised dash. The GT3 received an upgrade the following year and the extra 21bhp powered it to 190mph.

Finally, in 2004 a whole raft of new 996 flavours were let loose, including soft-top versions of the Turbo and the C4S. The Turbo S with 450bhp and standard ceramic brakes arrived to sit alongside a revised GT2 (with a power hike to 483bhp) and a 40th anniversary special edition C2. But for us the most significant of all was the GT3 RS, with further weight reductions, revised suspension, a full roll-cage and race seats.

DRIVING ONE TODAY
Comparing the 996 with its successor

After becoming acclimatised to the 997 the 996 now looks a little dated, a touch fussy in its appearance and even a tad heavy. It's amazing how things age once you become accustomed to a new look. Of course, it's far from ugly or awkward, it just appears that bit older, which is probably one of the reasons why prices have dipped so sharply.

Inside it doesn't have quite the quality of the newer car either, although it still feels tough enough to last forever. At least it's not over-burdened with buttons and switches, and the driving position feels slightly better, with the pedals ideally spaced for heel-and-toe downshifts. Make no mistake, it's still an excellent place to be.

On the move the 996 provides a slightly rawer driving experience than the 997. The engine feels superb – powerful in the mid-range, rising to a spine-tingling climax at maximum revs.

Over the past four decades every 911 incarnation has become smoother and more rounded, with the sensation of a heavy tail and light nose reducing each time. Moving back a model requires the driver to focus more on the messages the car sends. You have to settle the nose before unleashing the power. We are only talking degrees here, but you need to work that bit harder to extract the best from the 996. Some will say that this makes it the more involving car to drive. You learn something new about it on every journey, and by working with it you evolve new, subtle techniques for gaining the most from it.

It rides extremely well, displaying the kind of suppleness only a structurally stiff chassis can provide, soaking up the worst that UK roads can throw at it and never being knocked off its stride. Grip levels are impressively high too, and with all that weight on the rear tyres traction never becomes an issue. Cross country it would still be right there with the 997. Not bad for a car that costs way less than half as much.

Left: 996 C4S came oh-so-close in our 2002 Car of the Year contest (Honda's NSX-R just pipped it to the post). Above, from top: GT3, Turbo S and GT2

WHAT THEY SAID AT THE TIME

'I can't think of any other sports car that feels this *complete*. Every element has been honed. You can feel the quality and consistency of engineering in every control surface — steering, throttle, clutch, steering, brakes. There's a synergy here. Every component works together to create an exquisite, seamless whole'

– Peter Tomalin, evo 003, on the 996 Carrera

CHECKPOINTS

As always, a full service history is crucial. Ensure that all stamps are either from an approved Porsche Centre or a recognised specialist who has the official diagnostic equipment. Don't worry about high mileage cars, concentrate on condition. If the car has been used for trackdays ensure that service intervals have been reduced accordingly. Finally, check the VIN plate has a C16 country code, meaning that it's a UK car, not an import, as these can be very different in spec.

Bodywork/interior

There is a 10-year anti-rust warranty on 996s and they rarely show problems, except under the door catches on pre-2000 cars. Check underneath the car for signs of a misshapen floorpan, indicating that the car has been shunted. Interiors are hard wearing but can be prone to the odd rattle. On cabriolets the rear window can split in cold weather and it invariably means the whole roof needs replacing.

Engines

The main issue with 996 engines has been cracks appearing in the liners, resulting in hydraulic faults and the symptoms you'd expect to see with a blown head gasket. Specialists such as Autofarm (www. autofarm.co.uk) solve this by machining out the bad areas and fitting a bullet-proof lining. Also, intermediate shafts have been known to fail, causing the back

bearings to go. A stronger shaft has been developed, so once replaced the fault won't re-occur. Autofarm quotes £7500 for a full engine rebuild, including all the upgrades mentioned above, along with a chain tensioner upgrade and the fitting of a 997 rear main oil seal. Leaks from this seal are common, particularly if the owner has been using a thin oil such as Mobil 1. It's a minor issue as far as engine life is concerned, but it's a labour-intensive job to replace the seals and therefore expensive (about £1100). Look out for a film of oil on the rear end of the crank case. If the car has not run for some time it will sound rattly on start-up. Don't panic, if it settles down it'll just be the hydraulic valve lay adjusters, which need a coating of oil.

Gearbox

The transmission suffers few problems. The gearbox may feel sluggish when cold, but it will become slick once warm. There were some clutch failures on early cars, but these have mainly been resolved now. Expect at least 50,000 miles before replacement unless it has been abused. If you hear a knocking sound under load on the test drive it may be caused by a split driveshaft boot allowing dirt to get inside and break the joint.

Suspension

Other than wear on high-mileage cars, problems are rare. However, the geometry has to be spot-on and it can be knocked out by kerbing or hitting pot-holes. This can cost £250 to set up correctly. The

lower control arms should be examined for damage caused by grounding and the anti-roll bar bushes may need replacing on older cars.

Brakes/wheels/tyres

If the car has been used on track it's likely that harder brake pads will have been fitted, another clue to the use it has been subjected to. Tyres must have an N rating. These are approved Porsche tyres and the 'N' will be stamped on the sidewall. Pirelli, Michelin and Continental all produce tyres for the 996, although we prefer the Pirelli.

Values

Colour has a significant effect on values. Reds and yellows are hard to shift, while silvers and blacks are the most popular. Loud interiors are best avoided too.

In a private sale an average-mileage early car in a decent colour and in good condition will command around £15K, while the same car at a main dealer would cost closer to £17K. A 2000 model-year C2 will cost £22K privately and £25K at a main dealer, while a C4 will be about two grand more for a similar-age example. A GT3 from the same period will cost £35K in a private Top Marques ad, while a dealer will charge about £40K. An '03 Turbo demands between £65K and £68K, while a GT3 RS will set you back £64K.

If it's a rag-top you're after, a five-year-old C2 will cost around £18K and again the C4 commands a two-grand premium. A Targa from 2001 costs about £22K and a GT2 from 2003 would now cost you £50K, saving you £66K on the original new price.

MORE INFO

■ Porsche Club GB (porscheclubgb. com) offers technical advice to its members via regional contacts and a forum on its website. There is also a forum for Porsche enthusiasts at PistonHeads.com

The unmistakable 911 profile. Rear-mounted engine water-cooled for the first time in the 996. Can be prone to problems (see Checkpoints, above)

'I BOUGHT ONE' - MATT BAGLEY

'Anyone that knows me will tell you that I'm not that bright when it comes to cars. This intellectual blind-spot is especially dangerous as I change my cars a lot. In recent years TVRs, BMWs, Audis and Alfas have all had small holidays on my driveway, and although each has been great and totally different from the last, all along I've really wanted a Porsche.

'Now I finally have one and it's a beauty. After searching for several months for the exact spec I wanted, I eventually found the car you see here on eBay. I bought it outside of the auction for £28,500. It's been great so far. In fact I think I may even keep it for longer than three minutes!

'I cover up to 15,000 miles a year and use the car as a daily driver, but my insurance costs me £650 with THB Egger Lawson, which seems fair for a 32-year-old.

'It's hard to nit-pick about living with the car. It's very competent at everything it does. It's not thirsty and all of the aftermarket stuff that I would have wasted cash on has been done already, including £4000-worth of sports exhaust, which I could listen to all day long. I was a bit uncertain about the colour to begin with – I could hear my mates going on about it having 'a whiff of lavender' even before I bought it – but now I really love it.

'My one issue so far has been with the demister/heater control which only seems to want to create kiln or freezer conditions. It's a minor complaint, though.

'In short, I like my 996 a lot. It's great to finally own a Porsche!'

'If it's been on trackdays, make sure the service intervals have been reduced'

PARTS PRICES (for a 2000 Carrera 2)

Clutch kit	£464
Brake pad set front/rear	£82/£79
Damper front/rear	£340/£118
Headlight unit	£200
Windscreen	£464
Oil filter	£10
Air filter	£15
Starter motor	£300

SERVICING (Official Porsche Centre)

12,000 miles	£331
24,000 miles	£518
Annual service (for low mileage cars)	£151
Spark plug change (every 48,000 miles or 4 years)	£161
Brake fluid change (every 2 years)	£107

Servicing prices are for Carrera 2 '98–'01 model years

GROWING UP

In 2004, the new 997 was the most sophisticated 911 yet, but did it have the old magic? We drove the Carrera S, and put the regular Carrera through a group test (p80)

Take a moment, if you will, and put yourself in Porsche's position. Consider the corporate resolve, resourcefulness and sheer bloody-mindedness required to nurture the 911 through 41 years of continual development, to persevere with a fundamentally flawed layout that repeatedly forces you to find loopholes in the laws of physics.

Then, when you've got your head around that, imagine having those hard-won improvements, all that grit and graft, sniped at by successive generations of dyed-in-the-wool 911 enthusiasts who refuse to let go of the past. Loyalists so passionate they see virtue in the dynamic and ergonomic wrinkles that teams of dedicated engineers have spent years trying to iron-out.

It's a Porsche phenomenon. You don't hear Ferrari fans bemoaning the fact that the 575 Maranello doesn't possess the same Herculean controls of its ancestor, the Daytona. Nor do Aston Martin Vanquish owners feel cheated that their car doesn't weigh comfortably in excess of two tons and handle like a Panamanian oil

tanker, as the twin-supercharged V8 Vantage did before it. So why is it, if you're a fan of Porsche's enduring classic, that when the time comes to drive a brand new generation of 911 for the first time, you immediately think 'I really hope they haven't screwed it up'?

It's with a head full of such irrational, regressive logic that I board a Stuttgart-bound British Airways Airbus for an appointment with the all-singing Porsche 911 Carrera S. It's a momentous occasion, for regular readers will know how much we at **evo** love the 911. Whether it's the incomparable 2.7 RS of the early Seventies or the impeccable Carrera 4S of the Noughties, nothing in our experience consistently gets closer to epitomising what we look for in a driver's car.

And while this doubtless leads to many of you groaning when our Car of the Year comes around (thanks to Porsche victories in '98, '99, '00 and '03) our deep-seated affection for the 911 isn't unconditional. Magnificent though the C4S is, we placed it second to the Honda NSX-R in 2002's eCOTY. In 2001 we put the 996 Carrera way down the finishing order, and we gave the 996 ➔

GT2 such a lukewarm reception it didn't even merit inclusion in the year's biggest test.

On arrival at Zuffenhausen, famous home of the 911, a Guards red Carrera S sits waiting for me. As Porsche's design boss Harm Lagaay explains on page 98, after the enforced similarity of the Boxster and 996, re-establishing the 911's identity was a high-priority. Fortunately for Lagaay, with countless 996s parked in close proximity, the 997 is easy to distinguish. Broader, cleaner, *tighter*, it combines the presence of the current wide-bodied models with the understated individuality of the earlier 993 model.

As ever, what you make of the styling is purely personal, but if you're anything like me you'll take time to fully adjust to the changes. For instance, while I like the new frontal treatment, the mirrors and door handles look a bit fussy. Likewise the brash quartet of exhaust tail-pipes try a bit too hard to get your attention. Viewed as a whole, though, the 997 is undeniably handsome, individual and most importantly, unmistakably 911.

Grab that chunky door handle, pull open the door and you're looking at the most cohesive, well-constructed 911 interior ever. The door panels are slim, flat and beautifully simple. But the instruments, though clear, look too derivative. Crammed with switches for the stereo, ventilation, sat-nav and phone systems, the centre console is hellishly busy. Peppered with more than 50 separate buttons, it's the most graphic illustration of the 997's march into market territories as dependent on executive accoutrements as driving thrills.

There are other signs that Porsche is casting the 911's net a little wider with the 997. For the first time there's a choice of two normally-aspirated engines; the entry-level Carrera getting a 3.6-litre, 321bhp version of the familiar flat-six, the Carrera S getting a substantially re-worked, re-bored 350bhp, 3.8-litre motor.

Then there's the switchable suspension, active dampers offering a choice between comfort-biased compliance on normal setting and the 911's trademark iron-fisted damping when switched to sport. There's also variable-ratio steering, which retains the old car's ratio for the first 30 degrees of lock, then becomes increasingly direct as additional lock is applied. And finally there's the Sports Chrono pack, which in addition to the amusing dash-mounted analogue and digital stopwatch offers a Sport button that sharpens throttle response, raises the PSM stability control's intervention threshold and tenses the active damping.

Prior to my departure for Germany, much fat had been chewed at **evo** HQ about the 997's steering and suspension. Not only did such reliance on technology seem like a very un-Porsche thing to do, more worryingly we couldn't think of a single manufacturer that's made a convincing fist of applying such technology in a serious driver's car.

Despite the misgivings, edging through the security gates onto Porsche Strasse the early signs are all good. From the moment you twist the ignition key that big-bore engine delivers a reassuringly rasping soundtrack. Not as respiratory perhaps, but pleasingly deep and guttural nonetheless. The major controls have a honed, knowing uniformity of weight, from steering wheel to pedals and gearshift which, incidentally, swaps cogs in an all-new 'box developed to cope with the additional torque developed by the 3.8-litre engine.

Having spent my most recent 911 stints in a 996 GT3 RS, the suppleness of the Carrera S comes as something of a shock. You can sense the broad tyres shouldering their way over the urban lumps and bumps, but such is the control and pliancy few sharp-edged shocks get as far as the seat cushion: impressive stuff given the extreme width and low profile of the rubber. Perhaps there is something to this active damping after all.

As we break free of Stuttgart and slice onto the autobahn, the first chance to extend the 997 presents itself. Third gear selected, the tightly coiled feeder slip-road begins to unwind and I floor the throttle. With the instantaneous response of a big-capacity engine with low- ➲

While Porsche has looked to its past with the 997's design, resurrecting the classic oval headlamps last seen on the 993-series model, under the skin it features plenty of new technology, including variable-ratio steering and active damping. The 350bhp Carrera S (pictured) is blisteringly quick

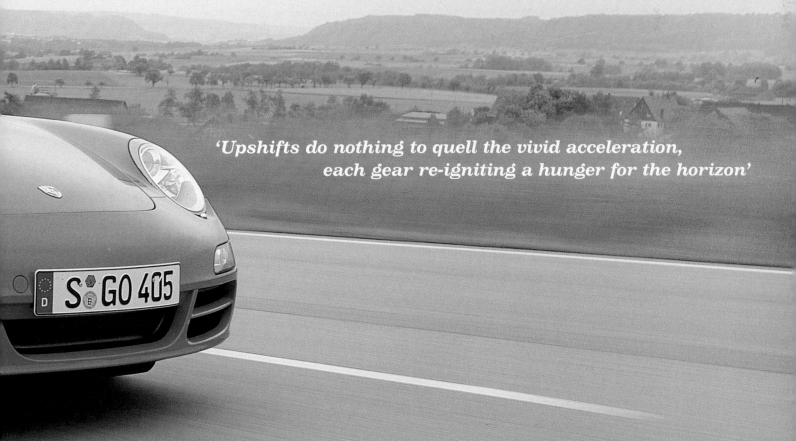

*'Upshifts do nothing to quell the vivid acceleration,
each gear re-igniting a hunger for the horizon'*

CARRERA DEVELOPMENT

Harm Lagaay has designed three generations of 911 and the 997 is his swansong model at Porsche

Few designers are presented with the opportunity to re-shape an icon. Fewer still, perhaps, are able to accept the challenge undaunted. Dutch-born Harm Lagaay has repeatedly relished the task, re-designing the 911 three times (993, 996 and now 997) during his two stints as the creative force behind Stuttgart's most famous car company.

With but a few weeks of his tenure remaining, **evo** paid a visit to his Weissach design office to gain an insight into the pressures of re-shaping Stuttgart's sacred sports car, and to discuss his Porsche swansong: the new 997 Carrera.

'The 911 is a very special design issue every time. It's iconic, of course, and it's very inspiring, too. The fact that it's an iconic car is not felt here because we are surrounded by it every day. We just accept it as it is. We love to do it and we are inspired by it. Everybody asks me "surely you have less freedom", but we don't feel that.

'All the designers who work on the exterior have the same opinion on how this car should evolve through the years. No-one complains about it being hard to change. There's no moment in time when we've said we're really scared to change it.

'Designing a new 911 is challenging, but it isn't hard in the same way it is to do a whole new car. The proportions are already there. Being typically 911, although the wheelbase has grown all the time, the proportions mean it has to retain a relatively short wheelbase with long overhangs.'

Looking back, designing the 996 version at the same time as the Boxster was a unique challenge, because the design team was tasked with creating two different cars that shared 33 per cent of their parts. The result, however, was the right platform strategy, which in turn gave the company the success that has brought financial freedom. And, thanks to that, it was a whole new situation a couple of years ago when work began on 997.

'Now we want much greater differentiation between the 911 and Boxster,' says Lagaay. 'That has given us more freedom and that is the reason why we said that for the 911 we should do something with a flavour of the earlier cars.

'I get nervous when people say the 997 is retro because it has 'round' headlights and 'hips'. It's definitely not retro! When I read in other publications that the car has more hips 'like the old days' I wonder what people mean because the old cars are actually very narrow. There are absolutely no hips until you get to the 993. Of course there were the Turbo models, but these had wheelarch extensions rather than hips. The common perception is that the car has always had hips, but this really isn't the case.

'Similarly, if you look at the headlamp closely you will see that it's not a round headlamp like the original cars, but a huge oval elliptic shape. It's extremely well executed and we put a massive amount of time into the details. Previously, designers that were in charge of headlamps would have just designed the shape, whereas now they design not just the shape but the whole unit. That's why all the inner shapes and textures now extend right up to the glass, rather than the more empty space you looked into with the 996.

'From day one we needed to have guidelines. In the end we settled on clarity, tension and precision. All three gave us the possibility to come up with a different sculptural feel, but we could also check every detail and make sure it created the right impression: Is it clear? Is it precise? Does it have more tension? These guidelines drove the approach to the whole car. I'm proud of individual elements such as the head and tail-lamps, but I'm most proud of the tautness of the surfaces. Even the fly-line of the roof coming from the windscreen down to the tail lamps – the typical 911 silhouette – has been made tauter; it's what gives the 997 its distinct character.

'Overall the 997 has been a fantastic project to run. If I look back on it, and I have been during my last few weeks here, it's been an almost perfect design process. It was a completely new way of developing a 911 compared to the 996, when things were very tight.

'I feel very relaxed about retiring. Of course there is much left to do at Porsche but the next cars that are coming out are going to be fantastic.'

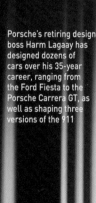

Porsche's retiring design boss Harm Lagaay has designed dozens of cars over his 35-year career, ranging from the Ford Fiesta to the Porsche Carrera GT, as well as shaping three versions of the 911

inertia internals, the 997 punches forward with tremendous force, engine note hardening with effort, steam-hammer torque melding with vibrant top-end zing. Upshifts do nothing to quell the vivid acceleration, each gear re-igniting a hunger for the horizon not dissimilar to the surreal 996 Turbo. One thing's for certain: no normally-aspirated 911 has ever felt this muscular.

Porsche claims the Carrera S will hit 62mph in 4.8sec, charge on to double that in 16.5sec and top-out at 182mph. That's major-league performance from 350bhp, and certainly enough to make the out-going 996 Carrera's formerly barrel-chested delivery feel comparatively thin.

Photographer Gus Gregory and I are searching for some quiet, winding and preferably hilly roads to challenge the 997's sophisticated chassis. Just as we're beginning to give up hope we strike lucky. Broad, wide and threading its way through dense woodland, the combination of long straights, fast fourth-gear sweepers and tighter, trickier third-gear bends is just what we need to test the 997's balance, poise, braking and traction. A rougher, less even surface would be a more complete test of its composure under pressure, but then there's no substitute for UK roads. The time for that will come in the Autumn.

Resisting the temptation to fiddle with the damper settings and the Sport and PSM buttons, I make my first few runs in 'Normal' with PSM engaged. With confidence and speed building, the 997's grip levels are clearly huge. Pleasingly it's hard to detect at which point the steering ratio begins to sharpen, but there's certainly no lack of directness or response, nor does it have the unpredictable rate of response that afflicts BMWs equipped with Active Steering. There is something missing though.

In the 996 (and previous models, come to that) you've always been able to gauge how hard you're pushing by the way the car nods its head. Coupled with the 911's inherent light nose and consequent reluctance to bite at the first turn of the steering wheel, you soon develop a subtle forearm shove technique to get the front-end working. The 997 doesn't ask that of you, but for that very reason nor does it give you your traditional reference points either.

For the next few runs I try switching the dampers into their firmer setting. The difference is subtle but perceptible, with more incisive turn-in and a more detailed stream of feedback flowing through the steering wheel. Engaging Sport is the final piece of the puzzle, providing an electronic shot of adrenalin through the 997's systems,

Subtle design tweaks at the rear include dropping the light clusters down into the bumper and reducing the number of slats on the engine cover. Carrera S identified by quad exhaust pipes (regular Carrera has just two). Below: interior is best of any 911

Specification

PORSCHE 911 Carrera S

○ Engine	Flat-six
○ Location	Rear, longitudinal
○ Displacement	3824cc
○ Cylinder block	Aluminium alloy
○ Cylinder head	Aluminium alloy, twin ohc, four valves per cylinder
○ Fuel and ignition	DME engine management, sequential multi-point fuel injection
○ Max power	350bhp @ 6600rpm
○ Max torque	295lb ft @ 4600rpm
○ Transmission	Six-speed manual, rear-wheel drive
○ Front suspension	MacPherson struts, coil springs, active dampers, anti-roll bar
○ Rear suspension	Multi-link, coil springs, active dampers, anti-roll bar
○ Steering	Variable-ratio rack and pinion, power-assisted
○ Brakes	Ventilated steel discs (330mm fr, 330mm r)
○ Wheels	8J x 19in fr, 11J x 19in r, aluminium alloy
○ Tyres	235/35 ZR19 fr, 295/30 ZR19 r, Michelin Pilot Sport N1
○ Weight (kerb)	1420kg
○ Power-to-weight	246bhp/ton
○ 0-62mph	4.8sec (claimed)
○ Max speed	182mph (claimed)
○ Insurance group	20
○ Price	£65,000
○ On sale	September 2004

evo RATING ★★★★★

sharpening its response further and bringing the final few per cent of cohesion to the dynamics.

It's funny how in isolation no one element makes a massive difference to the way the 997 feels or performs, but rather like turning up a dynamic dimmer switch, the Carrera S shines a little brighter as each stage is phased in. The bond might take longer to form, but the rewards are still there for the taking.

By the time we've exhausted the road's photographic potential, I'm pushing as hard as I dare, carrying crazy speed into the tighter corners with the fabulous brakes just on the point of locking, ABS giving the faintest tingle through the middle pedal, tyres chirruping in protest. As for PSM, well, it never so much as twitches, which either means I'm getting too old for this lark or the 997's limits are unlikely to be breached on the road.

Heading back towards Zuffenhausen, it occurs to me that what makes 911 enthusiasts so resentful of changes and improvements made to their sacred sports car is that mastering its foibles has long been held as a badge of honour; a driver's rite of passage, if you like.

Such folklore feeds on a degree of masochism and bravado, but such powerful emotions don't seem to sit comfortably in the 21st Century, and with each new generation of 911 the gnarly old purists' hard-won skills are rendered less and less relevant. As someone lucky enough (and old enough) to have lost their 911 cherry to a 964 Turbo, cut their teeth on 993s, really got to grips with the 996 range and filled in the gaps with models such as the 2.7 RS, 3.2 Club Sport

and 959, I can empathise. And I'm relieved to report that not only is the 997 significantly faster, grippier, more poised and more distinctive, but it could also never be anything other than a 911, either to look at or, more importantly, to drive. It's still a challenge too, but that has less to do with its legendary weight distribution and more to do with its limits being so bloody high.

The 997 is an awesome machine, a mighty achievement, and unless I'm proved wrong in the next few pages, the finest sub-£70K car on the planet. However, I'd be lying if I said part of me wasn't shedding a wistful tear as more of the 911's uniquely demanding character traits are erased. Same as it ever was, then.

Regular 997 Carrera rides on 18in wheels, although test car features optional 19in rims from more powerful S version. Chasing pack features current 996 911 Carrera 2, twin-turbo Noble M12 GTO-3R and BMW 645 Ci equipped with manual gearbox and Active Steering

ACID TEST

Just how good was the new 997-series 911? We pitted the regular 321bhp Carrera against BMW's impressive 645 Ci, Noble's searingly fast GTO-3R, and perhaps the toughest benchmark of all – the outgoing 996 Carrera

What on Earth do you take to meet the sixth-generation 911? It has no direct competitor; no other car maker is brave or foolish enough to take on the dynamic challenge of a rear-engined, 180mph sports car. It's an absurd concept, but as we all know, it works. 'Bloody well should after four decades of development,' snort the cynics. Well, yes, but every generation has worked, and has proved itself more than a match for its contemporaries, so there's no reason to think that the new 997 won't.

Which brings us back to that original question: what cars do you take the trouble to drive all the way from the UK to the middle of northern Germany in order to measure the ability and appeal of the latest 911?

The first is obvious – the current-generation 911, the 996, which in the UK steps aside for the 997 on September 18. But what else? Well, ed-at-large Meaden's early drive told us that the 997 is more fully equipped, more lavishly trimmed and features more technology, suggesting that Porsche fancies a bit of the market occupied by techno-packed, sportingly specced coupes such as the BMW 645 Ci. It also means that it might be leaving a gap for raw, simple, organic sports cars like the Noble GTO-3R. Three Channel Tunnel crossings are booked and a voyage of discovery is set in motion.

Time was when Porsche would launch a new 911 and for a year or more the only options to ponder would be colour, trim and wheel size. Not this time. Not only are there two models, the 321bhp Carrera and 350bhp Carrera S, but there are three distinct chassis configurations too: standard Carrera; Sport which is 20mm lower, stiffer and comes with a limited-slip differential; and PASM (Porsche Adaptive Suspension Management) which is 10mm lower and is standard on the Carrera S. We'd have liked a basic Carrera for this comparison but all the launch models are equipped with PASM which, like Sport, comes with 19in wheels and tyres.

Considering that the 997 is up to 80 per cent new compared with the 996, from behind the wheel it feels and sounds like business as usual; from the slightly bobbing nose to the raspy, guttural rumble of the flat-six behind. It couldn't be anything other than a 911. The gearshift of the new 'box is even ➔

Words: John Barker **Pictures:** Andy Morgan

Left: 997's interior a step on from 996 (above, right) in terms of quality and style, although centre console is a confusing mass of buttons. Manual gearbox feels even better than ever

better, all slack eradicated, giving an even crisper, more positive action, and the instruments are spread wider and look less cluttered. Not so the centre console. All 997s get the screen whether or not sat-nav is specified, which means that they all have the clutter of switches surrounding it.

The facia and cockpit design of the 996 has never been its most attractive feature, as I'm reminded when I meet up with our covert party. The new car's cabin is clearly of higher quality but what the old car does have is a simpler layout with a few larger, easy to find buttons for the rear wiper, heated rear window and PSM. Externally, the new car looks smoother and chunkier, especially from the rear three-quarters where its 11-inch wide, 19-inch diameter rims look massively tyred, almost cartoonishly so.

What I'm really keen to find out, though, is whether the new 997 really is as similar in feel to its predecessor as it seemed in isolation, so we head off in tandem to find some interesting roads, leaving the BMW and Noble behind.

An hour later, having discovered a demanding loop that includes possibly the worst road in Germany – its surface looks like a frozen sea – the new car has proved itself more stable and poised in virtually all situations. With every new generation of 911, the lightness of the nose and weightiness of the rear become less apparent, less dominant, and it's the case with the 997. The front of the new car holds up better and turn-in is more positive; there's less pitch and squat too, and even on rain-lashed sections there's so much traction and cornering grip that the stability

control warning light hardly ever flickers. No question, the effectiveness of the new car is very impressive.

What has always impressed us about the 996 is the feeling of structural integrity, the sense that no matter what a road throws at it, the suspension will always soak it up because the platform it works from is so stiff. Well, the 997 makes the older car's wheel control feel just a little less iron-fisted, and over that dreadfully lumpy road the older body seems to flex fractionally too. Elsewhere, the ride of the 996 seems marginally more supple. To go quickly you have to work a bit harder, waiting for the signals through the steering that the front tyres have settled into the turn before feeding in the power. Corner exit traction is sensational, of course, yet even on wet asphalt the enormous rear tyres of the new car find even more drive.

Apparently the Michelins developed for the 997 run at lower pressures, enhancing grip, but another reason the new car sticks to the road so determinedly is PASM. In default setting it is more supple than the standard 997 Carrera and at the push of a button becomes distinctly firmer and more sporty, but it's not simply a two-setting damper system. It is linked to sensors measuring steering rate, wheel motion, lateral acceleration, brake pressure and engine torque, and features response modes for scenarios such as a sudden lane change or emergency braking, automatically adjusting the damping force at each wheel for optimum control.

To judge by the 996, PASM certainly works, but the purist would say that the core driver appeal of the 911 is that it isn't perfect, that you've got to read what it's doing and tailor your driving to get the best from it. The argument that the new car isn't as involving or rewarding as the one it replaces is one that has been aired every time Porsche has evolved the 911. Is there anything more to it this time than nostalgia for the way things were? Perhaps. With PASM and 19in tyres, the 997 isn't quite as engaging as the stock 996 at moderate speed. There are a couple of areas where the older car is better, too; its pedal layout makes heel and toe downshifts easier, and its engine, although marginally less punchy at low revs, feels just as powerful and its note builds to a more thrilling crescendo.

Has the 997 moved too far towards being a mainstream coupe like the 645 Ci then? Absolutely and categorically not. The big BMW emits a wonderful, deep-chested V8 throb at idle and with 328bhp feels encouragingly brisk when you ➔

With 328bhp and rear-wheel drive, 645 should entertain on twisty roads, but nannying electronic systems spoil some of the fun. Below: 996 runs new Carrera close on performance – and sounds better at high revs

'The Noble's 352bhp is controlled solely by your right foot and the fat rear Bridgestones'

Above: twin exhaust pipes and absence of 'S' letter on engine cover are only visual clues this is not the 350bhp 997

coupe even though it's an auto.

There's no chance that the Noble will save you from yourself. The only time DSC, ESP, PSM, ABS and EBD have been seen at the Leicester works is in the annual Scrabble competition. The GTO-3R boasts 352bhp from its twin-turbo V6 and it's controlled solely by your right foot and the fat rear Bridgestones. Weighing just 1080kg, over 300kg less than the 997 Carrera, it ought to have the legs to leave the Porsche in its wake. It never quite happens, though.

The Noble smooths out the choppiest tarmac and corners strongly with rare poise, yet the yellow 911 is never far from its bumper. Partly this is because although its turbocharged engine delivers massive mid-range torque that allows it to stretch away on even short straights, the 911 exposes what lag there is, and partly because of the Noble's lack of anti-lock which means that you hold back, especially when the road is bumpy.

Outright pace isn't everything though – feel and feedback are perhaps more important in building driver satisfaction. Unfortunately for the Noble, the Porsche has got that covered, too, with steering that is every bit as accurate and brims with detail. As for the other controls, the GTO-3R simply can't compete – its throttle pedal wobbled around, its gearshift was vague and sticky and its brakes rumbled. In short, it didn't feel like a precision tool.

So, as expected, the sternest rival for the 997 is the 996. The new car does almost everything better while losing only a fraction of the older car's appeal, and I suspect a standard 997 Carrera with 18in wheels and without PASM will deliver more of the feel that 911 purists currently enjoy in the 996. However, the big seller in the UK is expected to be the Carrera S, which has PASM and 19s as standard. Oh, and the 350bhp engine, which is much faster and more thrilling than the 29bhp hike would suggest. In fact, an S with the sports suspension option and the excellent sports seats could well be the best permutation currently available. Think of it as a GT3 before Porsche gets around to it. ∎

prod the throttle. This example is also fitted with Active Steering which quickens the steering ratio at low speed for easier manoeuvring but is slower and weightier at speed so as not to over-excite the chassis. Clever stuff, but considering that the 645 Ci is made by the company that underlines its adverts with the slogan 'the ultimate driving machine', the Ci doesn't put much faith in driver ability.

There's not much feel through the steering and on a wet road the DSC stability control system is keen to the point that you feel it's being overly pessimistic about the level of grip available. Sure, a hefty and powerful rear-drive coupe could be a handful but DSC doesn't allow the Ci to flow. So you press the button for the required number of seconds to fully disengage it, intent on discovering the real 645 Ci, and you find that there's a final, impregnable layer of nannying.

Loop the lever of the slick six-speed manual 'box into second, turn for the apex, snap the throttle open and… the response just isn't there. The throttle pedal hits the stop but, being a fly-by-wire system, the car's computers can decide not to give you the power you requested. It's intensely frustrating and leads you to conclude that the chassis beneath you isn't much cop and you need to be protected from it. Perhaps we should have brought a Jaguar XKR, which rides better and is a more entertaining and engaging

	997	645 Ci	NOBLE	996
Engine	Flat-six, 3596cc	V8, 4398cc	V6, 2968cc, twin-turbo	Flat-six, 3596cc
Max power	321bhp @ 6800rpm	328bhp @ 6100rpm	352bhp @ 6200rpm	316bhp @ 6800rpm
Max torque	273lb ft @ 4250rpm	332lb ft @ 3600rpm	350lb ft @ 3500rpm	273lb ft @ 4250rpm
Power-to-weight	234bhp/ton	206bhp/ton	332bhp/ton	239bhp/ton
0-60mph	5.0sec (claimed)	5.5sec (claimed)	3.8sec (claimed)	5.1sec
Max speed	177mph (claimed)	155mph (limited)	170mph (claimed)	177mph (claimed)
Basic price	£58,380	£49,855	£49,950	£55,950
EVORATING	★★★★★	★★★★	★★★★	★★★★1/2

When you really need to stop.
Full stop.

Continental
Tyres – Engineered in Germany.

HELL CLIMB

Pikes Peak hill climb is a devilishly difficult 12.42-mile ascent with 156 corners. It requires courage – and a lack of imagination about the consequences of going off. We tackled it in a Cayenne ➔

Words: Richard Meaden | **Pictures:** Gus Gregory

Left: Meaden in action in the Cayenne. Far right: Meaden's instructor is Paul Dallenbach, who has won the event outright three times, racing his 800bhp open-wheeler. Right and below, views are literally breathtaking. You can see why the Pikes Peak hill climb is also known as 'The Race to the Clouds'

The Pikes Peak Highway is a road like no other. Stretching for 19 miles through the Pike National Forest in the wilds of Colorado, USA, this outrageous ribbon of asphalt and gravel has clung to the precipitous slopes of 'America's Mountain' for the past 88 years.

One of the world's highest roads, Pikes Peak Highway is open to the public on all but the most inhospitable days. In the course of a year some 300,000 tourists pay the $10 toll to make the dizzying drive to its oxygen-starved summit. Together with the 200,000 or so who ascend the mountain via the cog railway and a further 60,000 stout souls who make the arduous journey on foot or mountain bike, they make Pikes Peak second only in global popularity to Mount Fuji in Japan.

However, for a few days every year the tourist attraction becomes a motorsport Mecca, when the Pikes Peak Highway plays host to the most exhilarating driving challenge on the planet: The Pikes Peak International Hill Climb.

Packing a dizzying total of 156 turns into 12.42 miles of trail road, it's more Hell Climb than Hill Climb. Imagine lifting the Nürburgring's Nordschleife from the Eiffel region of Germany, screwing it up and throwing it at the side of a 14,110ft mountain and you've got some idea of the PPIHC course. And that's the nice bit.

Comprising predominantly a hard-packed gravel surface – the texture is a cross between a speedway track and a well-manicured forest rally stage – there are countless fresh-air drops awaiting those unfortunate enough to lose control. And there are no Armco barriers anywhere. Factor-in

unpredictable mountain weather that can pack all four seasons into the time it takes to reach the summit and you'll appreciate why former Indy 500 winners and World Rally Champions alike regard Pikes Peak as a unique challenge of skill and courage.

Racing driver or not, if you've got the merest drop of high-octane fuel in your blood, Pikes Peak is something of an ultimate. Ever since watching breathtaking footage of Ari Vatanen powering his Peugeot 405 T16 up the mountain in the film *Climb Dance*, I've wanted to experience the place first-hand.

To be honest it always seemed like a vain hope but, thanks to Porsche North America, for a small group of us that chance has come. And not only has Porsche managed to have the course closed to traffic, it has also enlisted four legendary Pikes Peak racers to act as our guides. Which is how I happen to be stood in the pre-dawn chill on the start-line of this incredible hill climb, shoulders hunched against the cold, stomach churning with apprehension and excitement.

With the mix of asphalt and gravel and steep gradients, Porsche has sagely identified Pikes Peak as the perfect proving ground for its multi-talented Cayenne Turbo. And while the purist in me is wishing it was a 911 instead, unleashing a 450bhp, all-wheel-drive Porsche on the world's toughest, most unforgiving hill climb course is a heart-pounding, mouth-parching prospect.

Working one-on-one with our instructors, we're to get just two goes at the mountain: one run

is to the half-way point to get a feel for the Cayenne and the surface, then we return to the start-line. There we'll collect our thoughts before embarking on a non-stop assault on the summit. My instructor is Paul Dallenbach, an experienced all-round racer who happens to be hooked on Pikes Peak. While he lacks the fame of one of the other instructors, the legendary multiple Pikes Peak and Indy 500 winner, Bobby Unser, I'm chuffed, for it was Dallenbach who stole Ari Vatanen's hill record to win outright in 1993, and who's also won outright in 2003 and 2004.

Chatting nervously before the off, I ask Dallenbach about the car he usually drives at Pikes Peak. What he says fills me with even more respect for his ability, not to mention his lack of imagination.

'It's a home-made rear-engined machine designed by an Indy Car engineer who was having a bit of fun. It runs in the open-wheel class and it's got a small-block Chevy V8 that's good for about 800bhp at sea-level. I guess you could say it goes a little…

'It uses old Indy Car parts (suspension, transmission, etc) but we took it and improved stuff, like the wings. With such limited development it's a case of trial and error with the aerodynamics. The only way we can test is on the back of a trailer going down the Highway.

'The wings are really big because the air is so thin up here. The higher you go the less downforce they generate. It's tricky to get the balance right between drag and downforce but

we're pretty happy with it now. Of course, you lose horsepower as you climb too, but the tyres deteriorate as well, so the car still gets slicker the higher you go. To be honest there's no real science to it. You just kinda go for it!'

Talking of which, it's time for us to start our first run, from the start-line to the half-way point at Glen Cove. It seems crazy to be accelerating hard along a winding, tree-lined and completely unfamiliar road in a two-ton-plus SUV, trusting implicitly the cool, informal pace-notes of a man I've only just met. But then my thoughts shift to Dallenbach and it doesn't take long to conclude that I've got by far the sweeter end of the deal.

The asphalt surface lasts for a mile or so before abruptly changing to hard, dusty gravel mid-corner. Dallenbach switched off the PSM system before the start, and it takes a second or so for

my jet-lagged brain to correct the inadvertent, momentum-fuelled slide the Cayenne has settled into. It's the first jolt of gut-wrenching adrenalin of the morning and it takes effect like intravenous Red Bull. Suddenly my still-sleepy nerve endings crackle into life, my eyes widen, palms begin to sweat and heart starts thumping as the seriousness of what we're attempting sinks in.

Despite the tricky under-Pirelli conditions, the Cayenne feels assured on the slick, talcum-powder-like surface. There's more feel and poise than you expect, and while I turn-in too hard for the first few switchbacks, by the time we get to Engineers Corner, Dallenbach's advice to try and pitch the Cayenne in on the brakes to get the tail swinging is starting to make sense.

We're approaching 10,000ft now, and though pulling strongly it's noticeable how hard the ◗

turbos are having to work to keep the V8 stoked in the vapid mountain air. Every lift of the throttle elicits a vocal *choo* from the turbo-chargers, every full-bore straight reveals the insidious creep of turbo-lag.

Under such relentless pressure it's almost impossible not to revert to what you know, and Dallenbach is constantly telling me to forget my circuit-style racing lines and get into the corners earlier. Invariably it's the tight line that proffers the most grip, but it's so hard to commit early to a blind corner when you know that all there is to catch your fall are a few pine trees.

More by luck than judgement we hit the sweet spot on the entry to Blue Sky, one of Pikes Peak's landmark corners. An endless, multi-apex left-hander that opens invitingly at the exit, we hook in on the tight line, then power all the way through with a half-turn of opposite-lock. It's a tremendously satisfying moment, but disturbing too, for it was achieved by putting total faith in Dallenbach's command to get hard on the power way before I could see through the corner.

We complete the run to Glen Cove, but the detail is fuzzed as my brain fries under the strain of reacting to Dallenbach's expert guidance and keeping pace with the Cayenne's needs. It's a thrilling, if somewhat sobering, introduction to the mountain.

On our way back down, Dallenbach senses my frazzled state and offers some reassurance that I'm only feeling how everyone who has ever raced at Pikes Peak feels after their first taste of the mountain. 'It takes about three years to feel you've learned it, but you need to do it in little sections. The best way to learn is to look at the landscape, to watch where the trees cut back.'

Back at the start, Jeff Zwart, a six-time class winner (five in Porsches) and another of our instructors, elaborates. 'This mountain is a 14,110ft living organism. It's constantly changing. From morning to morning the surface changes, the grip changes. It's a really interesting, complicated mountain.

'We've all come here and wanted to go fast, but you just can't learn it the first time. It takes a year of kinda simmering in your head before you can come back and prove you're beginning to know it. To go quick here you have to go way past what you can see, and it's that kind of knowledge that takes years to accumulate.

'I can remember one year, early in the first morning of practice back in 1994, Porsche Motorsport had loaned me a 550bhp turbo motor to drop into my 911 Carrera 4 lightweight. I was going into an area known as Picnic Ground and three things simultaneously entered my mind: One, this is Picnic Ground; Two, this is the earliest I've ever got into fifth gear here; and Three, this is NOT Picnic Ground! I guess that kinda illustrates my point about this place.'

With the sun rising fast and high, Dallenbach returns for our run to the summit. It's the moment of truth, and despite the trepidation of my first run, I'm hooked and raring to go.

Determined not to let my scant familiarity with the first half of the course breed contempt, I try to stay smooth and not push too hard through the few bits I remember. Recognising the approach to Blue Sky, I tense-up and fail to repeat the flukey, seamless line of the first run. Overall, though, I'm getting more comfortable with the surface and the Cayenne, and it feels as though we're carrying more speed.

'This mountain is a 14,110ft living organism. It's constantly changing'

The trick to being quick on Pikes Peak is to turn in to the corner long before you can see which way it goes – which requires either years of driving the hill, or having an old-hand alongside to tell you what to do. Even then, the total absence of Armco tends to play on your mind

That's the way to do it... Meaden powers the big Porsche around one of the loose-surface bends. Driving to the summit proved to be both nerve-racking and exhilarating

PEAK PERFORMERS

Top row, l to r: Bobby Unser in the '50s – the Unser family has made this event their own; rally star Per Eklund qualifying his Saab in 2002; this year's Unlimited class winner, Stig Blomqvist, in his 890bhp RS200. Middle row: when men were men – 1928 Packard 'Old Ironsides'; Louis Unser in the 60s, literally driving on the edge; in '92 Koichi Horiuchi mistook a hairpin for a gentle sweeper and went off the side at full throttle, cartwheeling several hundred feet down the mountain – his Mitsubishi was a mess, he walked away. Bottom row: the King of the Hill, Rod Millen, setting the all-time record of 10:04.06 in 1994 in his 1000bhp Celica; Millen again, in a Toyota Tacoma in 1999

Tarmac stops play

Pikes Peak may tower over the State of Colorado (at sunrise it casts a shadow 50 miles long), but even this mighty granite monolith is at the mercy of the most powerful force in the United States: litigation.

For many years the city of Colorado Springs was embroiled in a lawsuit instigated by the Sierra Club (a powerful body similar to our National Trust), which claimed that environmental damage (primarily pollution of the reservoirs near Pikes Peak) caused by soil erosion from the unmetalled Pikes Peak Highway violated the Clean Water Act.

In 1999 a court settlement was reached, in which the city agreed to implement a ten-year construction programme to stabilise the Pikes Peak Highway's surface. Almost three miles of unpaved track has subsequently been surfaced with asphalt, and it seems likely that the whole highway will now be paved to Federal standards, at a cost of more than $1million per mile.

Not only does this mean the end for Pikes Peak's famous gravel surface, but it will most likely mean Armco barriers and widening of the road to a uniform 30ft in width. It could even lead to some of the more severe gradients being softened.

Understandably, the PPIHC racers are dismayed at the irrevocable changes that are slowly but surely being imposed on their beloved road. While few drivers dispute that such erosion has an adverse effect on the water quality in the surrounding reservoirs and can harm vegetation growth, all point out that there are many thousands of miles of similarly unmetalled trail roads in Colorado. It just so happens that the dozen or so unpaved miles up Pikes Peak are the most famous. They also believe the familiarity of a hard surface and the psychological effect of the crash barriers will encourage drivers to travel too fast. And when the weather changes, as it does in the blink of an eye at such high altitude, a hail-storm, snow flurry or black ice will turn the asphalt road into a lethal skating rink.

Completion of the surfacing work is scheduled for 2012.

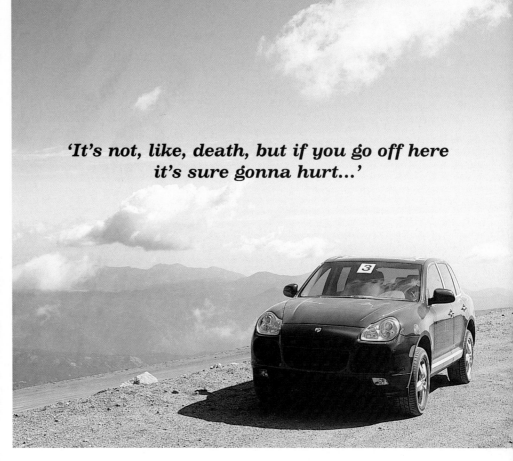

'It's not, like, death, but if you go off here it's sure gonna hurt...'

Beyond Glen Cove the incline steepens. More worryingly, as we breach 12,000ft we lose the trees and the misplaced reassurance that they give. Now there's nothing but sky.

The effect on your psyche is instant. Your muscles tense, your grip tightens and uncontrollable spasms of vertigo rack your chest. It's a genuinely horrid feeling. And all the time you're charging headlong up the mountain, your life literally held in your own hands.

With impeccable timing Dallenbach chimes in with an all-too-graphic pace-note. 'This is a straight called Ragged Edge. It's not, like, death, if you go off here, but it's sure gonna hurt...'

It's all been pretty high-speed stuff up until now, but after the pucker factor of Ragged Edge, the nadgety switchbacks of the section simply known as the 'Ws' are a welcome relief. It's a technical section of the course, though, and very easy to lose time through over-driving. The Cayenne doesn't like the tight hairpins, and for the first time you notice its hefty weight.

The relentless hairpins focus your attention so much you don't have time to scan the drops, but exiting the Ws and heading towards the Devil's Playground (so named because lightning often jumps from rock to rock during the region's spectacularly violent thunderstorms) that gut-wrenching feeling returns with a vengeance.

It's real big balls stuff from here to the summit, and I don't mind admitting that I can't bring myself to carry half as much speed through the long, blind sweepers as Dallenbach is telling me to. He clearly has far more faith in my ability than I do, but I daren't break my concentration for long enough to tell him so, and I'm reduced

to whimpering and stabbing at the wheel as we teeter on the edge of oblivion, rounding the aptly named Bottomless Pit, a 2000ft drop.

By the time we reach the summit my face is flushed, my hands are slick with cold sweat, brow moist from pure panic, legs quivering with adrenalin. It's been the most intense, all-consuming experience I think I've ever had: a stupefying cocktail of raw, judgement-blinding Blair Witch-style terror one minute, moments of clarity and total exhilaration the next. In a world obsessed with safety, blame and liability, Pikes Peak makes you feel alive. ■

Meet Art Walsh, as much a part of Pikes Peak as the dirt on the track. For the best part of 40 years, Art has waved the chequered flag at the top of the hill, with much enthusiasm; his son is now a start-line marshal. As for the natty tank-top, well, Art's mum knitted that for him

Soul
searching

In 997 guise the 911 was faster and more polished than ever before, but did it still have soul? To find out, we pitted it against a fabulous recreation of a classic early-'70s 911 ➔

Words: Jethro Bovingdon
Pictures: Andy Morgan

Porsche's new 997 has already become The Establishment – the car against which all others must be judged. In the wake of its arrival, supercars will have to work that bit harder to justify their stratospheric prices, hardcore sportscars like the Noble GTO-3R and TVR Tuscan will struggle not to look a little one-dimensional, and GTs like the Jaguar XKR and BMW 645i will do well not to look flabby and unfocused.

Game over? Well, not quite. For all its talent, speed and agility, the 997 shows some worrying signs of losing the ingredient at the very core of any 911's appeal. For 41 years the rear-engined Porsche has remained a unique challenge, a car that takes time to master but one that rewards so completely when you do that it has fired the imagination of generations of drivers.

For some the rear-engine configuration is a flaw, but if it is then it's a wonderful flaw because it defines the very essence of the 911. The first time you use the rear weight bias to kill understeer, feel the rear tyres taking the strain, and then unleash full power well before you think should be possible, you'll be a convert. Or maybe, if you're joining the 911 world for the first time with the new 997, you won't. Maybe the magic has gone.

With each successive generation the 911 gains even more grip, becomes more secure and less obviously rear-engined. Some have suggested that the 997 is perhaps a step too far; that it's evolved to such an extent that any tangible link in the driving experience with 911s of old has been severed. In short, that character has been erased in the name of progress.

We've already tested the 997 against its obvious rivals (evo 70) and it came out looking pretty invincible. Even its immediate predecessor, the 996, was overwhelmed. But the gradual erosion of character isn't the sort of thing you can easily spot. We need to look further back, to a time before ABS, PSM, EBD and PCCB to see if a purist's 911 can show up the 997 as a charlatan. What we need is a benchmark that's alive with that unique heavy-tail, light-nose 911 feel. A car that may not challenge the 997 in any measurable sense but one that may show it up in the more crucial areas that involve the driver: steering feel, chassis balance and buttock-clenching thrills.

Our search starts and ends at renowned Porsche specialist Autofarm, based near Bicester in Oxfordshire. They've been servicing, fettling and restoring 911s for 30 years and as good early cars become scarcer and more expensive they've found a neat solution for those who want that classic 911 look and feel with new-car reliability and integrity.

First they take the fully galvanised body of a 3.2 Carrera from the mid- to late-1980s and strip away the rubber bumpers and whale-tail spoilers to reveal an unadorned shell (911 bodies made from '72 to '88 are dimensionally all but identical). Any problems are rectified and once the shell is as-new, Autofarm fits new suspension, brakes, Fuchs alloys and the rebuilt and uprated (if requested) engine and 'box. The result is a perfect 911 that marries the corrosion protection and braking capabilities of a later car with the look and suspension geometry of something like the classic 1973 2.7RS.

Autofarm's demonstrator lacks the RS ducktail spoiler but looks fabulous: tiny, delicate and dripping with charisma. This is a sort of baseline car, designed to be everyday usable, and as such is fairly quiet and comfortable, but you can go as far down the lightweight route as your wallet allows. The price? Well, a car like this would set you back £60K. Or just £4500 less than our ceramic-braked, 321bhp, Sports-Pack-equipped 997 Carrera.

The drive from our Northamptonshire offices to Autofarm in the 997 is revealing. In fact the revelations begin even before you've climbed in. The new 911 looks compact and neat, modest even, and certainly less aggressive than the 996. It clearly draws inspiration from earlier models – the round headlights are the obvious 'classic' 911 signature, but the subtly pinched waist and shapely rear wings are similarly retro. Maybe Porsche has built a recreation of its own…

The new interior is more thoroughly detailed than the 996's and has some neat touches but somehow the architecture's a bit too ordinary, a bit too Cayenne-esque for my liking. Fortunately for 911 purists, the view out of the windscreen is still unmistakable and the 997, despite what I'd feared, feels narrow, threadable and unlike any other sports car.

The first thing to say, though, is that the 997, even this regular 321bhp model, is devastatingly quick. Fast in a straight line without ever being intimidating, it's when the road gets gnarled and challenging that the 997 seems to find another level of speed. There's huge grip front and rear and that big 3.6-litre flat-six hung out the back affords enormous traction even in sopping wet conditions. It's a creamy power unit too, delivering from way ●

Latest 997 version of Porsche's rear-engined sports car feels sublime on these sort of roads, but is it too sterile? Autofarm's gorgeous recreation of a 1970s RS-style 911 is beautifully detailed (below). The two cars cost virtually the same, so it's a valid comparison test

information that flows through the 997's wheel. This wasn't in the script…

But that's not to say the Autofarm RS doesn't have a lot going for it. For starters it's modern-car quick, lugging nicely from about 2500rpm and really kicking at the top end; the ride is superb and shrugs off even the nastiest British B-road with ease, and despite the obvious repercussions of taking liberties with an older 911, it never feels eager to spit you off the road. By any standards it's an engaging, enchanting car to hustle, suffering only from a slight lack of body control over crests and when you begin to really lean on the period-looking but modern construction Michelin Pilot Exaltos.

Understeer is well controlled but inevitable and you don't feel inclined to push much further or bring the heavy tail swinging into action, simply because the idea of sorting out any oversteer on the road, in an old 911, is a scary prospect. A real RS is probably close to 200kg lighter and feels scalpel-sharp in every sense compared with this 'comfort'-spec recreation. We'd want to strip out more weight, add power and noise, sharpen-up throttle response and tie-down the body a bit better, all of which is possible thanks to Autofarm's extensive options list.

The harsh reality, though, is that the 997 does everything better than the older car, and not just the obvious things. Take it as read that it's in a different world in terms of sheer speed, but the real achievement is that the modern car is simply more communicative, more visceral and you can exploit more of its potential more of the time. Better still, despite having limits you might think would be impossible to enjoy at road speeds, the opposite is true. It feels so well balanced and so responsive to steering, throttle and brake that you can revel in the experience even at sane speeds.

And when you do want to go hard the 997 allows you to access all of the benefits of having a rear-mounted engine without any of the potential downsides. There's no snappy on-limit behaviour and you feel liberated from the fear of irrevocable momentum oversteer. The brilliantly judged PSM stability system even gives you complete confidence on roads running with water. It's a 911 with all the feel, character and involvement you could want and it's on your side, always. The older 911 is another easily taken scalp for the 997. It seems technology need not erode dynamism and driver enjoyment after all. ∎

down low and then closing in on 7000rpm with a greedy fervour. The more potent 350bhp Carrera S must be mighty.

In short, the 997, here without the PASM adjustable dampers, feels every inch the 911. The noise is straight out of the textbook, and any dry-yowl cliché doesn't quite do it justice. And then there's the steering, which is different from any 911 that has gone before it, losing much of the chatter and tug that you'd expect, but still sublime. The way it seems to transmit fine detail about the road surface straight to your nerve endings is remarkable. But best of all the 997 still shifts its balance underneath you depending on your throttle inputs, still needs help to fulfil its huge potential, and from the driver's seat still feels incredibly malleable.

I arrive at Autofarm wide-eyed, but the 997's crushing display evaporates from my mind when the RS Re-creation rolls out. It's immaculate, it's gorgeous, and the key is soon in my hand. After drinking in the purity of the shape I drop into the seat and get a shocking reminder of pre-996 Porsche cabin design and ergonomics. 'Charming' is probably the best word to describe it, although 'terrible' might suffice. The pedals are offset to the left, the ugly steering wheel feels too big and the gearbox is loose, vague and long of throw. It really is tiny in here too, yet although it feels like I've stepped back in time, the compactness and low seating position feel perfect for serious driving.

Interestingly, the air-cooled 3.2-litre 231bhp engine is decidedly quiet and the noise itself isn't a patch on the 997. Hmm. It doesn't have that instant response that makes the 2.7RS so thrilling, either. The narrow, bumpy lane that leads from Autofarm's facility brings another shock. Where the stiffly sprung 997 tugged and weaved, steering jigging this way and that, the unassisted and slower-racked RS Re-creation simply drives straight and true, with no fuss but not much in the way of feel, either.

Out on the fast roads nearby, that famed bobbing nose returns and the steering starts to writhe with information, but it never matches the clarity of

	AUTOFARM 911	PORSCHE 997
○ **Engine**	Flat-six, 12v	Flat-six, 24v
○ **Location**	Rear, longitudinal	Rear, longitudinal
○ **Displacement**	3164cc	3596cc
○ **Max power**	231bhp @ 5900rpm	321bhp @ 6800rpm
○ **Max torque**	210lb ft @ 4800rpm	273lb ft @ 4250rpm
○ **Kerb weight**	1180kg	1395kg
○ **Power-to-weight**	199bhp/ton	234bhp/ton
○ **Wheels/tyres**	7 x 15in fr, 9 x 15in rr, alloy. 205/50 ZR15 fr, 225/50 ZR15 rr	8 x 18in fr, 10 x 18in rr, alloy. 235/40 ZR18 fr, 265/40 ZR18 rr
○ **0-60mph**	5.8sec (claimed)	5.0sec (claimed)
○ **Top speed**	150mph-plus (claimed)	177mph (claimed)
○ **Price as tested**	£60,000	£64,497
evo RATING	★★★★	★★★★★

PORSCHE 917

Was there ever a more dramatic-looking racing car than the 917 long-tail?
Fast but an absolute handful, it evolved into one of the all-time greats

MARTINI
RACING - TEAM

MARTINI INTERNATIONAL CLUB
MARTINI & ROSSI

PORSCHE

PORSC

BILSTEIN | Firestone
SHOCK ABSORBERS | TIRES

Words Roger Green | **Pictures** Porsche Museum

Stunningly beautiful low-drag lines and a starring role in Steve McQueen's cult movie, *Le Mans,* are just two reasons why the 917 has attained iconic status. But for the men behind the machine neither of these things mattered; the desire to win was all-consuming.

It's hard to believe now, but before the 917 hit the track Porsche was never anything other than the underdog in sportscar racing. The Zuffenhausen factory had never won Le Mans outright and through the Sixties it had been comprehensively trounced by both Ferrari and Ford. At Porsche there was a steely determination that this state of affairs would not be allowed to continue into a new decade, and no expense would be spared in the pursuit of victory – even if it meant building 25 complete cars to comply with homologation rules.

Based on the fast but ultimately fragile 908, the new chassis frames for the 917 were ultra-light – just 42kg – and because the design team wanted the new car to be as compact as possible the driver was positioned so far forwards his feet were ahead of the front axle and therefore effectively part of the crash structure. Behind this brave soul was a 4.5-litre flat-12, basically two flat-sixes back-to-back, which initially produced 520bhp, easily enough to propel the 800kg car to the far side 200mph. It was, to put it bluntly, a rocketship with the driver protection of a paper bag.

The early outings for the 917 weren't exactly covered in glory. In fact the car was so difficult to drive – the first long-tails actually produced lift, creating terrible instability – that at the Spa 1000km in 1969, factory drivers Brian Redman and Jo Siffert decided to drive the old 908 instead. Three weeks later the story was the same at the Nürburgring, so (because the factory needed publicity to sell off the

homologation cars) David Piper and Frank Gardner were drafted in at short notice to drive the tricky long-tail. They brought the car home in an unspectacular eighth place.

Not that it was ever dull in the cockpit. Piper today recalls it as 'a lethal weapon that flicked around like an ox-tail and generally tried to kill you'. It was so bad they had to leave a huge margin for error at every corner to ensure they got to the finish. Things were no better for the drivers at the 1969 Le Mans 24hrs and yet despite this the 917s had a 30mph advantage over the rest of the field on the Mulsanne and set an extraordinary pole time that was over 12 seconds faster than the previous year.

To drive like Rolf Stommelen did on that occasion required raw courage: danger was never far away. The first 917 privateer, John Woolfe ,who admitted to being scared by it,

'To drive like Stommelen did required raw courage. Danger was never far away…'

paid the ultimate price at Maison Blanche on the opening lap of the race. His car ran wide, crashed and exploded into flames and poor Woolfe succumbed to his injuries. Despite leading by almost 50 miles, the works entry retired with a gearbox failure with just three hours to run.

Derek Bell, who went on to win Le Mans five times, began his long association with Porsche driving the 917. In fact it was his acceptance of its wayward high-speed nature that won him a seat in the team. Bell takes up the story: 'The test was at Goodwood, my home circuit, and there were three of us in contention for the drive: me, Ronnie Peterson and Peter Gethin. I got the nod and for years I thought it was driving talent that won the day, but chatting to Gethin recently I discovered that wasn't entirely true. The 917's unpredictability had terrified both him and Ronnie and basically scared them off!

'At that stage the 917 was still at an early point in its development – it was all over the place – but with my experience of the Ferrari

Martini was one of
Porsche's favoured
racing teams and
enjoyed much success
with the 917. This is
a 1971 917LH (LH
standing for *langheck*
or long-tail). Drivers
might have preferred
a longer nose
section...

'For 1971, designer Robert Choulet produced

THE BALANCE
OF POWER

Which is the better driver's car, a top-spec Boxster S or a basic 997 Carrera? We put them head-to-head on road and track, with surprising results ➔

Words: John Barker Pictures: Andy Morgan

'We get to discover whether a £38K Boxster can deliver the thrills of a £58K Carrera'

For once, I'm giving nothing away when I reveal that a Porsche wins this twin-test. Question is, which one? Since its launch, the new 997-generation 911 has engaged in a non-stop round of 'meet and beat', taking on and seeing off a variety of rivals. Most recently the new C6 Corvette failed to get the better of the Carrera, and before that our biggest-ever Car of the Year contest was won by the Carrera S.

So, yes, we're big fans of the new 911 but we're not blinkered – we think the new Boxster is outstanding, too, and if we'd had our way, eCOTY would have hosted a more balanced Porsche in-fight. Instead of stock 231bhp Boxster against 350bhp Carrera S, the top-spec Boxster S would have met the standard Carrera.

Well, now they do meet, and we get to discover whether a £38K Boxster S with a few well-chosen options can deliver the thrills and satisfaction of the £58K Carrera. We'll drive them on road and track, and for a broader perspective on their abilities they'll be assessed by two drivers of differing experience: **evo** columnist and 911 novice Richard Porter, and me.

It's a more even contest than the £20K price difference might suggest. In fact, it's difficult to see why their prices are so far apart. It's not as though the Boxster is a smaller car or stuck with a clunky four-cylinder engine. Like the 911 it has a flat-six, a 3.2-litre that pumps out 276bhp, just 45bhp less than the Carrera's 3.6, and it could be argued that the Boxster is the purer sports car.

It doesn't have rear seats like the 911 but that's because its engine is mid-mounted rather than slung beyond the rear axle, giving superior weight distribution. Its versatility comes in the form of a neat electric folding roof and decent boot space.

The options fitted to our Boxster S include 19in wheels and tyres and the excellent Porsche Active Suspension Management (PASM). Available on a Boxster for the first time, PASM upgrades the chassis with computer-controlled active dampers, allowing a supple ride to be combined with firm suspension control when it matters. You can also specify Porsche Ceramic Composite Brakes (PCCBs) but this car wasn't fitted with them.

Our Carrera is the most standard on Porsche GB's test fleet and comes with 18in wheels and suspension that doesn't have the optional PASM dampers. Even so, it's a chassis that represents the culmination of decades of development and fine-tuning to capitalise on the advantages of the rear-engine layout. It's fitted with PCCBs, but has no other secret options.

So, in the red corner, the car that's been 40-odd years in the making, the archetypal driver's Porsche, the iconic 911 Carrera. And in the yellow corner, the young pretender, the mid-engined maestro, the Boxster S. Place your bets…

TECHNICAL COMPARISON

The significant differences between the 997 Carrera and Boxster S are engine position and body type, the rear-engined 911 being a coupe and the mid-engined Boxster an open-topped roadster. Despite the extra strengthening needed to ensure the Boxster's body is sufficiently rigid, at 1345kg the Boxster S is 50kg lighter than the 997 Carrera. It is also shorter by 100mm (3.9in) but its wheelbase is 65mm (2.6in) longer, which helps its weight distribution – its mass is split 45/55 front/rear compared with 38/62 in the Carrera.

Chassis-wise, the Boxster S and Carrera have identical brakes as standard, with 318mm (12.52in) vented discs up front and 299mm (11.77in) vented discs astern. However, while the Boxster has MacPherson strut suspension all round, the 997 marries MacPherson struts with a five-link configuration at the rear, allowing greater tuning of wheel control. PSM stability control is standard on both, as are identical tyres on 18in rims.

The flat-sixes of the Boxster and 911 are technically similar – aluminium block and heads, dry-sump lubrication and four valves per cylinder with variable valve timing – but are unrelated. The Boxster's bespoke engine is physically smaller and has its gearbox mounted behind. The 3179cc version arrived in 2000 and its output has risen from 252 to the current 276bhp, with peak torque of 236lb ft. The Carrera's 3596cc flat-six is slightly more efficient and develops 321bhp and 273lb ft, which ensures it has the better power-to-weight ratio – 234bhp/ton versus 208. ➔

UNDER THE SKIN

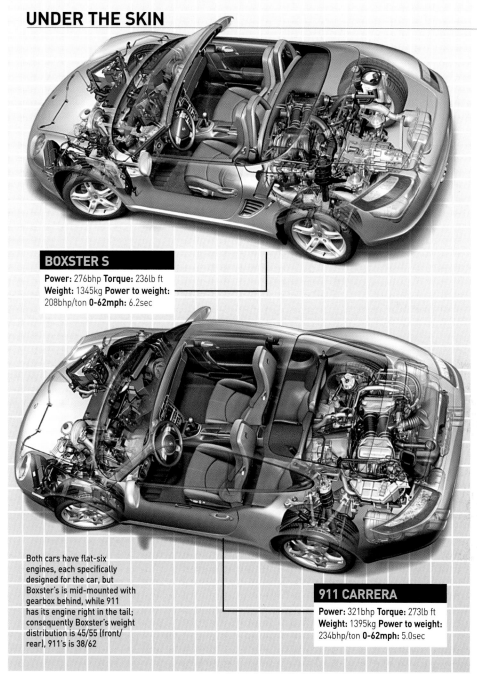

BOXSTER S
Power: 276bhp **Torque:** 236lb ft
Weight: 1345kg **Power to weight:** 208bhp/ton **0-62mph:** 6.2sec

Both cars have flat-six engines, each specifically designed for the car, but Boxster's is mid-mounted with gearbox behind, while 911 has its engine right in the tail; consequently Boxster's weight distribution is 45/55 (front/rear), 911's is 38/62

911 CARRERA
Power: 321bhp **Torque:** 273lb ft
Weight: 1395kg **Power to weight:** 234bhp/ton **0-62mph:** 5.0sec

THE 911 NOVICE'S VIEW BY RICHARD PORTER

ON THE ROAD

The talented Mr Barker is in the 911 and the untalented Mr Porter is following in the Boxster. Bumpy, sinuous roads like this are a tough test, especially for a butter-fingered fool, and yet immediately the mid-engined Porsche is on my side. The wheel shimmies and writhes, but it's all pure, useful information from the front tyres, while the car itself tracks straight and true. The body control is astonishing. On roads like these some sports cars would force you to back off, but there's never a hint of this – and I'm keeping the 911's plump bum in range. On longer straights big brother's extra 45bhp allows it to pull away, but the advantage is cancelled out at the next corner. For a rank amateur like me, the Boxster's handling is simply terrific. No hint of the front end pushing on, no pant-wetting suggestion that the rear is about to break loose. Even doing something dumb like backing off mid-corner provokes only a gentle sensation of sideways weight transfer that disappears as soon as you step on it. Only once do I have a slithery moment, after hoofing the throttle too early out of a slimy bend. I'd like to claim it was my natural opp-lock ability that sorted it but in truth the car just dug in and recovered itself, without troubling the stability control. The Boxster made me feel like a God.

Switch to the 911 and everything seems familiar yet unsettlingly different, like returning to an old school, or wondering what the dentist has done to your back teeth. It takes just a couple of corners to know that, where the Boxster was my faithful friend, the 911 carries the faint hint that it might want to kill me. That feeling of weight transfer you get in the yellow car only by being daft, it's there all the time in this. Is it psychological, a nagging bit of my cowardly brain that's saying 'rear-engined cars are scary', and if it is, did Porsche have to contribute to it by making the steering lighter? In some ways the rear-engined car is better than its sibling, notably the carbon brakes and the mechanical chunkiness to the gearchange, but they're not enough to offset the way it has eroded my confidence. Unsurprisingly,

Barker in the Boxster builds up quite a lead and by the end of our road route my conclusion is simple. In a mild way I'm mistrustful of the 911. Whereas I want to marry the Boxster.

ON THE TRACK

A few scrappy laps in the 911 and the real surprise is that, even with some really oafish behaviour, its arse will not swing loose and scare the life out of me. At least, not before the PSM has stepped in. The disappointment is how much understeer there is. Barker politely avoids asking if I know what an apex is, and offers some advice on braking points, racing lines and use of power. And suddenly something remarkable happens. The 911 comes alive. That rear-engined layout isn't the widowmaker it felt on the road; it's there to press down on the rear wheels, mashing them into the track as you get back on the gas, giving the grip to punch you out of corners. Treat the 911 properly and it'll return the favour and then some. I've misjudged this car; it is truly intoxicating.

Back to my first love, the Boxster. I'm hoping its on-road confidence will translate onto the track. Putting the engine in the middle certainly means less understeer, and there's no hint of weight right at the back as you turn into the sharper corners, but the Boxster's more friendly nature is actually its downfall here, even for a skills vacuum like me. You can whip round in a decent time, but there's no real edge to it, no feeling that getting it right will reward you. I admit I left both cars in 'sport' mode so that the PSM remained on partial duty. And again, the Boxster felt like it was letting the family down. In the 911, the computer lets you get mildly out of sorts and gives you a chance to extract yourself from the mess before stepping in. The Boxster's techno guardian is simply over-zealous. It was still fun, but it couldn't reach the giddying, endorphin-soaked pleasure of nailing the 911 through a corner just so.

The Boxster feels built for instant gratification – the 911 you have to get to know. And when you do, it gives a sense of satisfaction even its wonderful brother can't possibly match.

ON THE ROAD

It's a damp, grey, mucky old day, the sort that sheens the tarmac with a slippery film. Not pleasant but useful for revealing handling traits at sane road speeds. Our road driving will include a half-hour circular route that takes in both fast A-roads and bumpy, challenging B-roads, with the faster stuff first. To give Porter a less intimidating start, I lead in the 911.

The integrity, the sense of solidity that a 911 exudes is one of its most appealing and enduring characteristics. It feels built to handle its performance, almost over-engineered for the job, yet at the same time it interacts delicately with the road surface and sends a detailed stream of information to the driver about how it's going down at the tread-blocks. The light nose/heavy tail is immediately apparent but if you've driven a few you almost subconsciously adopt the traditional 'slow in, fast out' technique to make the most of the traction. Even on a day like today, the drive the Carrera finds is astounding. At successive corners you try harder but the tail stays glued. The PASM-equipped Carrera launch cars were quite different, seemingly conjuring up a chunk more front-end grip and bite to match the traction, but somehow they were a fraction less involving.

If you haven't driven a 3.8 Carrera S, the 'regular' 321bhp 3.6 flat-six is sensational, with a thrilling, escalating delivery and howl. It's a classic noise, a stirring, whirring rumble that's as intrinsic a part of the 911 experience as the weight distribution and the low-slung, narrow cockpit. The gearshift is sublime, the lever slicing with great feel and precision across the gate, and the powerful carbon-composite brakes give a superb pedal that's firm right from the top of its travel yet progressive and easily modulated.

Yup, I'm having a great time at the wheel of the Carrera, well into the groove. And I'm impressed by Porter's pace in the Boxster; its yellow nose is ever present in the 911's rearview mirror.

Onto the bumpier B-road section, the mildly bobbing nose of the 911 becomes less keyed-in and in a couple of moderate-speed corners the nose washes out a little. Keep a steady throttle and turn a fraction more and the nose tucks in to bring the car back on line. It would be foolhardy to switch off PSM stability control and try to unsettle the rear to tighten the line.

Swap into the Boxster and you notice only subtle differences in outlook – lower roof, different dash, slightly lower seating position, or is that psychological? There's a similar relaxed rumble from behind and, surprisingly, not a great deal of difference in their low-speed demeanour. Fine ride quality, slightly weightier, talkative steering and the feeling that there's more weight

Barker found Carrera the more confidence-inspiring of the two, revelling in its fantastic levels of feedback and superb traction coming out of corners; Boxster can snap sideways if you dish up too much torque in corners, but Porter found he went much faster on the road in the mid-engined car

'Boxster is ever present in the rearview mirror'

behind than in front. The contrasts reveal themselves when you wind up the Boxster's flat-six, which isn't nearly so exciting. Its note is whinier and there are no exciting stages where the delivery ramps up as the 911's does. It's as though the Boxster is heavier and is smothering its engine's sparkiness. This is a deception, though; allowing for speedo error, at the end of the straights the Boxster is hitting almost the same numbers as the 911 was.

This time, though, Porter isn't in close company; he dropped away from the Boxster's rump after the first sequence of challenging bends. I can see where his confidence in the Boxster came from, but only up to a point, and that point is the peachy 90-degree-plus second-gear corner which the 911 had romped away from with all 273lb ft harnessed. The Boxster snaps and slithers sideways as the torque arrives, which

catches me by surprise. The stability control seems to be caught unawares, too.

Whereas my confidence had built and built in the 911, this moment undermines my confidence in the Boxster. What's specifically uncomfortable, for me, is that the front end is so resolute in its grip. You turn and the nose tacks crisply into the turn, giving no hint that the surface won't take anything like full throttle. What about in quick sweeps – is the tail going to go first there, too? Onto the B-road section, the Boxster's stronger front-end bite is noticeable at the corners where the 911 gently understeered, and, impressively, over the difficult lumps and bumps its structure feels almost as solid as the 911's.

I was more comfortable with the Carrera but, having seen Porter's pace in the Boxster and how quickly he had dropped behind in the 911, I suspect he feels differently… ➔

'Boxster doesn't have the same degree of mechanical traction'

ON THE TRACK

Both Porter and I were convinced we had lapped the West Circuit at the Bedford Autodrome faster in the 911 than we had in the Boxster. A stiff breeze and weak sunshine had dried the surface before we recorded our lap times, and the 911's superior power-to-weight made it feel much punchier. On track you get to hold full throttle for a lot longer than you would on the road, and it felt like the 911 was arriving at the corners at much higher speed than the Boxster. Also, it seemed to have crisper pick-up away from the corners.

The Carrera has so much natural mechanical grip that it rarely troubled the PSM system. In the faster corners it adopted a mild understeering attitude, and even unsettling the tail slightly for sharper turn-in for the two fast corners at the end of the lap (with PSM off), the tail slipped and recovered with smooth progression.

The Boxster immediately felt slower, mainly because its engine doesn't have the sparkle of the 911's. The mid-engined car doesn't have the

same degree of mechanical traction either, the rear more eager to slip out of line getting away from the tighter turns. For my laps I had PASM in its 'sport' setting, giving stiffer dampers and significantly backed-off stability control but it was still cutting the power at the exit of the tight bus-stop chicane, Pif-Paf, so I turned it off altogether.

One thing that was evident from the early exploratory laps was that when you provoke the 911's tail into large oversteer, out of the hairpin for instance, there's a point of no return: keep on the throttle and it spins; back off and it spins. The Boxster will go to the same angle and come back again if you're precise with the throttle.

The data confounded our subjective assessment, however. Although the 911 did indeed attain higher peak speeds, it wasn't nearly as good at getting into the corners as the Boxster. This is probably partly due to the mid-engined car's better weight distribution and partly due to the PASM suspension resisting dive up to the turn-in point and roll once it has turned. The

911's (optional) carbon composite brakes didn't give it any advantage in outright deceleration but resisted fade more completely than the Boxster's steel disc set-up, which had shown an uncharacteristically soft feel on the road. The net result is that for both Porter and myself, the Boxster was marginally faster over the lap, by 0.1sec and 0.3sec respectively, and we were more consistently quick in it, too. ➔

We were as surprised as anyone when the data showed that both Barker and Porter were quicker on track in the Boxster

911's superior power-to-weight ratio makes it feel quicker around Bedford's West Circuit. It's a determined understeerer (right) until you find its natural rhythm. Ultimately the 911 hits higher peak speeds, but proves less effective at getting through the corners quickly

STANDARD v PASM
TONY BAILEY

I was intrigued to compare my own PASM-equipped Carrera S with the 'basic' Carrera. Suspension in standard mode, PSM stability control fully engaged, my S is an impressive thing, but PSM does hamper fluid cornering at the limit, taking control of the car's responses too early and frustrating any efforts to explore and utilise the chassis' ultimate adjustability.

Selecting 'sport' mode – which knocks the PSM back by 50 per cent – but leaving the suspension on standard gives you close to full rein, allowing full-blooded drifts through Palmer Curves, O'Rouge and the like. Putting the suspension on its firm setting results in even better turn-in and stability during direction changes and gives the car a more track-orientated feel. Turning PSM off completely would appear to be pointless.

Initially the standard car seems lighter and more fluid in its responses – probably due to its smaller wheels and lighter ceramic brakes – but under harder braking its composure slips, and the nose dips, hampering turn in and revealing understeer. It's more eager to kick its tail out earlier too, and once at a decent angle requires more driver input to hold it there.

Biggest surprise is that the ceramic brakes on the non-PASM car seem inferior to the standard ones on mine – probably down to the suspension. Braking over undulations into turns, the red car is all chirping tyres and flashing ABS light while the PASM car is more composed and able to brake later despite arriving at higher speed. We didn't time my car, but PASM alone allows later braking, sharper turn-in at higher speed and earlier application of power so it's going to be quicker – and as much fun with PSM de-armed.

If you're considering a standard 997 add PASM before ceramic brakes. Buy an 'S' with PASM as standard and neither the Boxster S nor the standard 997 will see which way you went.

BOXSTER v 911 – BARKER v PORTER

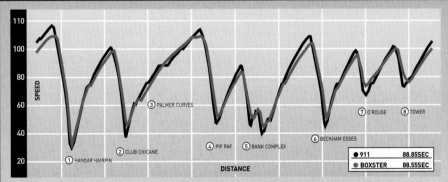

| | 911 | 88.85SEC |
| | BOXSTER | 88.55SEC |

▲ Barker's track chart: The trace clearly shows the performance advantage of the 911, but equally illustrates the Boxster's superior front-end grip; John quicker into all of the corners in the mid-engined Boxster but arriving at the next at a higher speed in the 911. The Boxster seems more stable through the very fast Palmer Curves, too.

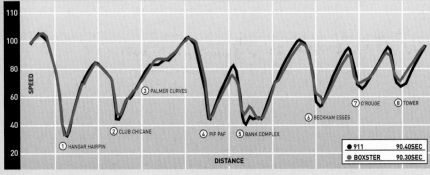

| | 911 | 90.40SEC |
| | BOXSTER | 90.30SEC |

▲ Porter's track chart: Richard clearly not as confident in either car, but essentially his traces follow the same pattern as John's, with higher turn-in speeds in the Boxster, the 911 clawing much of the deficit back on the straights. He's actually quicker than JB into the slow corners, which tends to create big understeer. That's working at Top Gear for you...

Hit the button marked 'sport' and the PSM is knocked back by 50 per cent, allowing more on-track fluidity

SPECIFICATION

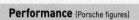

	BOXSTER S	911 CARRERA
■ Engine	Flat-six	Flat-six
■ Location	Mid, longitudinal	Rear, longitudinal
■ Displacement	3179cc	3596cc
■ Bore/stroke	93/78	96/82.8
■ Compression ratio	11.0:1	11.3:1
■ Block	Aluminium alloy	Aluminium alloy
■ Cylinder head	Aluminium alloy, dohc per bank, four valves per cyl, vari valve timing	Aluminium alloy, dohc per bank, four valves per cyl, vari valve timing
■ Max power	276bhp @ 6200rpm	321bhp @6800rpm
■ Max Torque	236lb ft @ 4700-6000rpm	273lb ft @ 4250rpm
■ Transmission	Six-speed manual	Six-speed manual
■ Front suspension	MacPherson struts	MacPherson struts
■ Rear suspension	MacPherson struts	Five-link, coil springs
■ Steering	Rack and pinion, PAS, variable rate	Rack and pinion, PAS, variable rate
■ Brakes *optional	Vented discs all round, ABS, PSM	Vented discs all round, Carbon Composite*, ABS, PSM
■ Wheels *optional	8 x 19in fr*, 11 x 19in rr*	8 x 18in fr, 10 x18in rr
■ Tyres	235/35 ZR19 fr*, 265/35 ZR19 rr* Michelin Pilot Sport	235/40 ZR18 fr, 265/40 ZR18rr Michelin Pilot Sport
■ Weight	1345kg	1395kg
■ Power-to-weight	208bhp/ton	234bhp/ton
■ Basic price	£38,720	£58,380
■ As tested	£41,268 (inc. 19in wheels/tyres, PASM and leather sports seats)	£63,729 (inc. Carbon Composite brakes)

Performance (Porsche figures)

■ 0-62mph (100kmh)	6.2sec	5.0sec
■ 0-100mph (160kmh)	12.3sec	11.0sec
■ Standing km	24.9sec	23.8sec
■ Max speed	166mph	177mph

EVO RATING	★★★★★	★★★★★

Even up against the awesome talent of the PASM-equipped Boxster S, the 997 Carrera still emerges as a uniquely rewarding experience. It's a car that's greater than the sum of its parts. But it didn't have things all its own way, and less experienced drivers would almost certainly enjoy the Boxster more

VERDICT

We love the new 911. We love the new Boxster. We rate them both as five-star, best-in-class driver's cars because they are so capable and characterful. So, which would we have? Richard Porter, a virtual 911 virgin before this test, sums it up thus: 'Which to choose? Well it's a real world of greasy B-roads and dark, wet motorways out there so I think I'd be very happy with the Boxster, up until the point I started craving more power and a bigger challenge. Then I'd chop it in for a 911 and a track-day season ticket. I'm the Porsche marketing department's dream, I am.'

For me, it's the 911. It's the more exciting of the two, thanks to its power delivery, and the more engaging thanks to its unusual weight distribution. Sure, technically it's not as capable as the PASM-equipped Boxster S, as the track session showed, but that's not something that ever bothers you driving on the road. Also, the 911 communicates better what's happening under the tyres.

If you intend taking a Carrera on a few track days, PASM would be valuable for the better body control and understeer suppression it offers. Those active dampers would also enhance the Carrera's on-road ability but you've got to ask how fast you really want to go. Isn't it a good thing to have more than sufficient grip while still enjoying the feeling that it's mostly you rather than the car that's in the driving seat from turn-in to apex to next straight?

If you'd never driven a 911, you'd be very satisfied with the Boxster S. It shares all of the more expensive Porsche's qualities, only some, such as the unique engine sound, are present in slightly smaller doses. The Boxster wins group tests for the same reasons the 911 does; for its brilliantly honed dynamics and feel, finely judged ride and handling compromise (even less of a handling compromise with PASM), and its reassuring integrity. But I know that if I had £60K to spend on a new Porsche and I chose the Boxster S, I'd regret the decision every time I saw a Carrera. ■

DMS 535D
"LAUGH-OUT-LOUD FAST"
EVO JUNE '05

DMS 996 TURBO
"NOT ONLY IS THERE STAGGERING TORQUE,
THE POWER IS UTTERLY ADDICTIVE"
AUTOCAR JULY '04

DMS 330CD
"NEW ECU MAKES THE CAR SO MUCH FASTER
YOU SIMPLY HAVE TO HAVE IT!"
AUTOCAR OCT '04

DMS 996 TURBO
"STUPENDOUS EXPLOITABLE PERFORMANCE"
EVO AUG '04

DMS 997 TURBO
"MIGHTY IMPRESSIVE.
SEEMLESSLY IMPROVES THE TURBO'S BEST ASSET"
EVO MAY '07

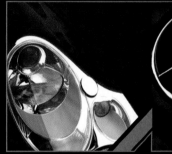

PORSCHE
997 TURBO » 540+ BHP
996 TURBO/GT2 » 550+ BHP
997 CARRERA S » 376+ BHP
997 CARRERA » 348 BHP
996 GT3 » UP TO 400 BHP
996 3.6 » 344 BHP
NEW BOXSTER S » 300+ BHP
CAYMAN S » 317 BHP
CAYENNE S » 366 BHP
CAYENNE TURBO » 522 BHP
2007 CAYENNE MODELS &
997 GT3 » IN DEVELOPMENT

MERCEDES-BENZ
SL65 AMG » 650 BHP +DE-LIMIT
AMG55 KOMPRESSOR » 550+ BHP
AMG 55 » FULL DE-LIMIT
CL63 AMG » 562 BHP
& DE-LIMIT (RE-MAP AND LOWER
ABC SUSPENSION)
CL600 BI-TURBO » 558 BHP
SLK55 AMG » 389 BHP
SLK 350 » 297 BHP
ML420 CDi » 368 BHP
NEW S/ML320 CDi V6 » 274 BHP

BMW
M5 V10 » 548 BHP 205MPH
M3 E46 » 370 BHP & DE-LIMIT
M3 CSL » 372 BHP & DE-LIMIT
335i » IN DEVELOPMENT
650i » 398 BHP & DE-LIMIT
330D E90 » 276+ BHP
320D E90 » 209 BHP
330D E46 » 260+ BHP
X5 3.0D » 260 BHP
535D/335D » 334 BHP

EXOTIC & MISC
FERRARI 430 » 525 BHP
FERRARI 360 » 440+ BHP
MASERATI GRANSPORT
& QUATTROPORTE » 438 BHP
AUDI RS4 » 439 BHP & DE-LIMIT
RANGE ROVER TD6 » 226 BHP
R ROVER SPORT TDV8 » 328 BHP
R ROVER SPORT 2.7D » 232 BHP
VW TOUREG V10 TDi » 365 BHP
BENTLEY CGT/F-SPUR » 620 BHP

ALL OTHER CARS PLEASE CALL US

WORLDWIDE OFFICES AND INSTALLATION:
UK » IRELAND » EUROPE » USA » ASIA » AUSTRALIA
SINCE 1997

0845 850 1845   SALES@DMSAUTOMOTIVE.COM   WWW.DMSAUTOMOTIVE.COM

In 2005 the new mid-engined Cayman posed a threat to even the mighty 911. We found out just how good it was, with a little help from a classic 993 ➲

Emergency

911?

To save on development and production costs, the Cayman's interior (left) is pretty much the same as the Boxster's, except for the mesh atop the instrument binnacle. Behind the seats is a carpeted luggage-stowage area rather than the Boxster's lidded hood-storage compartment

Ten minutes after loading camera bags and luggage into the Cayman and closing the tailgate, I make a telling slip. We're stuck in roadworks, the sun is already hot in the clear morning sky, and I reach for the catch on the header rail that releases the folding roof. Only there isn't one, because we're not in a Boxster…

It's an error I make only once. By the time we return the Cayman to the factory in Zuffenhausen later that day, the character and ability of the new coupe are firmly established in my mind. I reckon it's right up there with the best Porsches I've driven.

When details of the Cayman were first released, I wasn't at all convinced that a Boxster-based coupe was the thing to fill the gap between the Boxster S and basic 911. What's the point when the Boxster does such a good job of being the 911's understudy? It offers much of the 911's character, handles superbly, is remarkably practical and – almost as a bonus – features a very tidy folding roof. We discovered just how well it handles when we pitched Boxster S against regular 911 on road and track back in issue 077. Objectively there was little between them, and although we thought we'd driven the 911 faster around the track, it was the Boxster (equipped with PASM, ceramic brakes and 19in rims, and still £15K cheaper) that posted the fastest laps.

Still, our conclusion was that, if we had the money, we'd buy the 911, mainly for its more exciting power delivery, unique dynamics and greater sense of involvement.

Put a tin roof on the Boxster and it could be argued that you diminish rather than widen its appeal. Of course you'd expect Michael Baumann, boss of PR at Porsche, to demur and, over dinner the evening before we drive the new car, he does. 'The 911 sells to people who know what the car stands for and can afford it,' he says. 'The Cayman is a driver's Porsche aimed at younger buyers who may be unaware of the 911's heritage.'

It's a thought-provoking statement. Many of us have grown up promising ourselves that one day we'll own a 911, but there's a generation that hasn't seen Porsche's most glorious motorsport successes, or the many competition-shaped but still obviously 911-based derivatives that have triumphed on track. That generation may see the 911 as an anachronism, or perhaps simply isn't quite ready for it. Also, the pinnacle of Porsche's recent supercar history is the Carrera GT, a car that is mid- rather than rear-engined.

Against that backdrop, the idea that the Cayman is a 911 for drivers on a smaller budget makes sense. However, anyone who really wants a 911 would surely look at the price of the Cayman S (almost £44,000), trawl the classified ads and realise that they could spend almost £20K less on a 993 Carrera and get the same performance. And we mean the same: there are striking parallels between the Cayman S and the 911 of a decade ago. The Cayman's 3.4-litre flat-six makes 291bhp and 251lb ft (Carrera 285bhp

Even though the Cayman S and 993 are near-identical in size, power and weight, it still comes as a bit of a shock to discover just how hard it is to shake off the older car

'What strikes me is how impressively supple the Cayman is'

and 251lb ft from 3.6 litres), drives through a six-speed 'box (ditto) and propels the car's 1340kg (1370kg) to 62mph in 5.4sec and on to a top speed of 171mph, same as the Carrera.

Indeed, so compelling were the parallels that we hunted down a fit example of the last of the air-cooled 911s, wrote a cheque for it, and then drove it all the way to southern Germany to meet the Cayman, intrigued to see what a difference a decade makes. As I collected the key to 'our' Cayman S at the factory, our 993 was up in the hills an hour west of Stuttgart,

waiting for the confrontation.

Those who'd already seen the Cayman in the metal told me that it looked much better than in photos, and they were right. Whether by chance or design, the Cayman was backed up to a flight of five or six steps, giving us an elevated view of its most distinctive angle. For me, the rump of the Boxster has always been its best aspect and the long slope of tailgate accentuates the curve of the hips over the rear wheels. Styling is, of course, entirely subjective. The profile is less happy to my eye – every time I trace the line

from the nose I expect it to finish with a fuller, rounder 911 tail. Maybe I'll get used to it. Also, a couple of the details look a little contrived – the vertical strakes for the side vents and the high-set spots in the intakes either side of the number plate.

Structural integrity is one of the reasons the Cayman can be an even more focused driver's car than the Boxster. From the outset the Boxster was designed to be a convertible, so the platform underpinning the Cayman is already pretty solid. The addition of a fixed metal roof ties the structure together and creates a substantially more solid shell. Porsche says that in terms of flexural stiffness the Cayman is 100 per cent improved over the Boxster, and in terms of torsional stiffness is almost a match for the 911.

This means that firmer springs and tighter dampers can be used and the dynamics can be more finely honed, giving the opportunity to make the Cayman a more serious driver's car, a car more like the 911. Yet what strikes me within the first few city miles is how impressively supple the Cayman is. A solid platform benefits ride just as it does handling – it's all about wheel control.

'At the hairpin, the Cayman's power could edge the car sideways'

may keep up in a drag race but would quickly lose ground over twisting, bumpy tarmac. The Cayman is a more serious rival for the current 911 than the Boxster, and it's all down to structural integrity. Good as the Boxster's handling is, the more solid shell of the Cayman has allowed finer suspension tuning and enabled the advantage of the mid-engined layout to be more fully exploited. It's a shame we weren't also able to try a standard Cayman S to gauge the contribution PASM makes.

The price still doesn't quite add up for me, though. Convertibles are generally more expensive than coupes because of the extra engineering that goes into them and the costly roof mechanism, yet the Cayman S will cost £43,930 compared with £38,720 for the Boxster S. It's almost as if the car has been priced so that it fits into the gap between Boxster S and basic 911. Even so, I'd take Cayman over Boxster every time. Besides being dynamically more precise and polished, it has a more characterful and peppier engine and also the best brake feel of just about anything I've ever driven.

Versus current 911? That's trickier. On paper it's virtually as fast as the 321bhp Carrera, and the engine shoving it along has inherited some of the 911's character along with its cylinder heads. It doesn't handle like a 911 but I've a feeling if we repeated the Boxster/911 comparison test with the Cayman, the Carrera would feel pretty ponderous and significantly slower on track. Speed isn't everything, of course, but if you don't buy into the 911 heritage, the Cayman looks a bit of a bargain, even at £44K.

SPECIFICATION

	CAYMAN S	993-SERIES 911
■ **Engine**	Horizontally-opposed 6-cyl	Horizontally-opposed 6-cyl
■ **Location**	Mid, longitudinal	Rear, longitudinal
■ **Displacement**	3386cc	3600cc
■ **Cylinder block**	Aluminium alloy, dry-sumped	Aluminium alloy, dry-sumped
■ **Cylinder head**	Aluminium alloy, dohc per bank, 4v per cyl, VarioCam Plus variable inlet cam timing	Aluminium alloy, sohc per bank, 2v per cyl, VarioRam variable inlet manifold
■ **Fuel and ignition**	DME engine management, sequential multipoint fuel injection	Bosch Motronic 5.2 engine management and fuel injection
■ **Max power**	291bhp @ 6200rpm	285bhp @ 6100rpm
■ **Max torque**	251lb ft @ 4400rpm	251lb ft @ 5250rpm
■ **Transmission**	Six-speed manual, rear-wheel drive, PASM	Six-speed manual, rear-wheel drive
■ **Front suspension**	Double wishbones, coil springs, PASM damping system, arb	MacPherson struts, coil springs, anti-roll bar
■ **Rear suspension**	Double wishbones, coil springs, PASM damping system, arb	Double wishbones, coil springs, dampers, anti-roll bar
■ **Steering**	Rack and pinion, power-assisted	Rack and pinion, power-assisted
■ **Brakes**	Cross-drilled and vented discs, 318mm fr, 299mm rr, ABS, PSM	Ventilated discs, 304mm front and rear, ABS
■ **Wheels (as tested)**	8.5 x 19in front, 9.5 x 19in rear	7.0 x 17in front, 9.0 x 17in rear
■ **Tyres**	235/35 ZR19 fr, 265/35 ZR19 rr	205/50 ZR17 fr, 225/40 ZR17 rr
■ **Weight (kerb)**	1340kg	1370kg
■ **Power-to-weight**	220bhp per ton	211bhp per ton
■ **0-62mph**	5.4sec (claimed)	5.4sec (claimed)
■ **Top speed**	171mph (claimed)	171mph (claimed)
■ **Basic price**	£43,930	£61,250 (in 1996) £79,122 adjusted to 2006 prices
EVO RATING	★★★★★	★★★★★

993's air-cooled flat-six displays the patina of its 80,000 miles, yet it still performs with satisfying vigour. Soundtrack's more muted than fond memory suggests, but still unmistakably Porsche

Nardo, Italy, December 2004: the small team from Dortmund-based Porsche tuners 9ff are hard at work fettling their extraordinary 9F-V400. It's based on the mechanicals of the turbocharged GT2, heavily modified and shoehorned inside the shell from the narrower-bodied GT3

Perfect

weapon

With over 400bhp
and the heart and
soul of a racecar,
in 2006 the all-new
GT3 was primed to
tear holes out of
the opposition ➲

The GT3 is a weapon. Speed, precision, consistency and feedback are all that count, and it lives by its mission statement with unswerving commitment. Which means it isn't for everyone. But if you crave purity of purpose, engineering excellence and sheer excitement then the 997 GT3 is an all-consuming drug.

There have been mutterings amongst the Porsche hardcore that the new GT3 might be a bit 'soft'; it's the first extreme 911 fitted with traction control, Porsche Active Suspension Management (PASM), the option of sat nav and even cupholders. But from the soles of its super-sticky and meticulously developed Michelin Pilot Sport Cup boots (there will also be a GT3-specific Pirelli P Zero Corsa tyre offered), to the tip of its downforce-inducing rear wing, the GT3 is wonderfully single-minded.

Beyond the adoption of PASM, the GT3 has familiar but substantially revised hardware under the aggressive new sheet metal. Hung out behind the rear axle is the revered dry-sump 3.6-litre flat-six that has graced GT1, GT2, Turbo, GT3 and GT3RS in one guise or another over the past decade. It's much stronger than the new flat-six found in the Carrera and Carrera S, and in the new GT3 it seems to rev forever.

Porsche has eked-out an extra 28bhp from the already high specific output engine, taking the total to a mighty 409bhp. Indeed, the obsessive weight-saving within the engine itself and the quest for more horsepower are perhaps the clearest indications of just how serious this new GT3 really is.

Completely new or thoroughly revised in every detail save the crankcase, the new engine is known in Porsche circles as 'The Masterpiece'. Examples of the engineers' obsessive striving for the absolute optimum include longer titanium connecting rods that reduce internal friction, forged pistons and smaller diameter gudgeon pins that save 30 grams per cylinder, and the crankshaft itself, which is now lighter by 600 grams thanks to an improved forging process.

Tiny savings, but together with lighter valves and hollow-cast camshafts, bigger throttle butterflies and a variable-length intake manifold, they enable the engine to rev to 8400rpm, 200rpm up on the 996 GT3. Ram air scoops on the engine cover build up over-pressure in the intake system and further aid combustion, while the compression ratio has risen from 11.7:1 to 12.0:1. The result is that phenomenal 409bhp at 7600rpm. Which is 114bhp per litre. Power isn't at the expense of torque either, the GT3 thumping out 298lb ft at 5500rpm.

Combined with gearing 15 per cent shorter

Above: PASM suspension soaks up bumps but still feels beautifully connected. Bucket seats are from Carrera GT. Classic 3.6-litre dry-sump flat-six now good for 409bhp

than the previous GT3 (and 22 per cent shorter than a Carrera) it's no surprise that the performance claims are little short of outrageous. Hook-up the flat-six perfectly off the line and, according to Porsche's usually conservative claims, you'll be past 100kph (62mph) in 4.3sec, 100mph in 8.7sec (a figure we couldn't match even in the 505bhp Corvette Z06 last month), and 124mph in 13.5. Flat out, the GT3 is good for 192mph. These are proper supercar numbers. At £79,540, the GT3 almost looks like a bargain.

Those startling figures are due in part to the GT3's kerbweight of 1395kg. On paper that makes it 15kg heavier than the last model, but the figures are skewed because the old model didn't have air-con as standard. The new GT3 does, and it accounts for a hefty 20kg. Consider too that the new shell (a hybrid sharing much of its body-in-white with the stiffer, wide-body C4/Turbo, but with the more slippery Carrera/S skin) is 8 per cent stiffer torsionally, while flexural stiffness is up a significant 40 per cent.

Aluminium doors and bonnet and a composite plastic engine cover help. Even the bigger 19-inch wheels are no heavier than the old 18-inch items. You'd almost feel guilty not speccing the ➡

'On tight, narrow
and dusty roads
in the hills around
Verona, the GT3
simply flows'

£5800 PCCB ceramic brakes, which are a full 20kg lighter than the standard set-up.

Of course there's much more; a Porsche engineer could write a book on the technology that's been applied obsessively to make the GT3 so utterly ballistic. But head of the GT3 programme and serious petrolhead Andreas Preuninger (official title: Project Manager High Performance Cars, which must keep him pretty busy) sums up the GT3 without a single cold, hard engineering fact. 'The GT3 is pure emotion. Nobody needs a GT3, not many people will drive it every single day, but when you want to really drive, this car is awesome.' Time I found out for myself...

My GT3 is fitted with the ClubSport package, which means my hips are pinched by carbonfibre buckets (borrowed from the Carrera GT, they weigh just 10kg each), while the rear-view mirror is full of criss-crossing rollcage. It's a no-cost option, and a no-brainer as far as I'm concerned.

The Alcantara-rimmed steering wheel and gearshifter add to the no-nonsense feel of the GT3, and when you twist the ignition and the flat-six wakes-up with a grumpy, agitated idle, your senses tingle with anticipation. You sit very low, and instinctively you pull the steering wheel as close as you can. When you're letting the GT3 off the leash you just know it'll be important to have a tight grip on the wheel...

Having said that, for a car that looks like it'd happily contest Le Mans with the simple addition of some race numbers, the first thing that strikes you is just how easy the GT3 is to drive. The steering shares its variable-ratio rack with the Carrera and feels very similar. It tugs a little more for your attention due to the broad, stiff-sidewalled 235/35 ZR19 front rubber, but it's beautifully weighted and always pulsating with information. Flicking between the gears requires more effort than in a standard 911, or even the previous GT3. The shift is much shorter, but the action is a touch stiff. Even so, it's sweeter and slicker than, for example, the shift of an Aston V8 Vantage. But it's the ride quality that feels most at odds with this GT3's racebred roots.

The adoption of PASM has allowed Porsche to really hone the damping for two opposing ➔

Walter Röhrl

IT'S A CREDIT TO PORSCHE'S PR machine that Walter Röhrl has become more renowned as the man who hones 911s, Boxsters and Caymans on the Nürburgring than as a double world rally champion, and it almost seems a cliché to talk about the hand of genius that has clearly touched the GT3.

As we trundle out of the pitlane of the Adria race circuit, near Venice in Italy, I suspect that Röhrl is about to show why Porsche is so keen to make that connection. Sure enough, the circuit that I've just driven as quickly as I'd dare suddenly becomes an entirely different place. His lines are less conventional but clearly much quicker and the speed he carries from turn-in to the apex is deeply unsettling.

The cornering and braking forces feel brutal in the pit of your stomach, but Röhrl is so calm and smooth that the car itself seems to be floating around the track. He likes the GT3 then? 'It is a fantastic car, and the way it manages to be both better on the road and much faster on the track is incredible,' he answers, the pace barely diminishing.

Röhrl has helped develop the new Turbo (which we'll drive next month) in parallel with the GT3 and is best placed to evaluate their divergent characters. 'It's a very different car. If you like to drive on tracks or even on good roads the GT3 is more... *fun*. Lighter, more responsive.' As if to demonstrate, the GT3 is pitched sideways and smokes out of the next turn, riding high on the kerbs. 'Around the Nürburgring I expect they'll be around the same time, though. The Turbo's traction is unbelievable and for everyday driving it is the best.'

Röhrl makes no apologies for the addition of traction control on this GT3. 'The system is very good – in slow corners the car has such great traction anyway that it rarely activates (the first lap is with traction on, and even at Walter-pace it's notable by its absence). This is a very, very fast car and I think traction control is great for when you're not fully concentrating.' And how will it affect the time at the 'Ring? 'Maybe two seconds a lap faster without, because in the faster turns sometimes a bit of slip is good.'

The GT3 still hasn't set a definitive lap time at the Nürburgring, but Röhrl is confident it will comfortably eclipse the previous GT3 and even the GT3RS. 'I think five seconds quicker is easy, probably seven or eight seconds quicker than the RS – and that did a 7:47.' And the new RS? 'That depends on how much weight they get out of it, but I think another two seconds quicker again.' That could put the time as low as 7:38. For reference, a Carrera GT's time is 7:32.44...

Andreas Preuninger

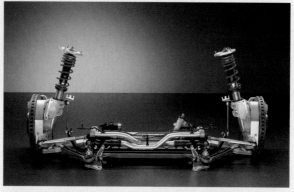

'PROJECT MANAGER HIGH Performance Cars'. Now that's what I call a job title. Although it's a little disturbing that there might be a 'Project Manager Low Performance Cars', or something similar, at Porsche. Maybe the person in question only works one day a week, and isn't invited to any of the strategy meetings...

Andreas Preuninger has the look of a man who works eight days a week, and when you're charged with developing a car as iconic as the GT3 it's easy to understand how it could become a bit of an obsession. Preuninger is clearly a man who enjoys his job. 'We spent probably 10,000km on the 'Ring finalising the damper settings,' he says. 'It was hell...'

On a serious note, it's incredible just how important the Nürburgring has become for Porsche. Preuninger explains, 'The Nürburgring is everything. It is *everything*. We must go quicker there with the new car, but it's the surface, the variety, that makes it so important to get things like damping right. If it works there you have the whole world covered.'

Select the stiffest PASM setting and the new GT3 isn't tailored to the 'Ring. 'This setting is very stiff,' says Preuninger. 'Great for somewhere like Hockenheim, but the standard setting is

quicker on most roads and on the Nordschleife.' He is incredibly animated whenever he's talking about the GT3, and is perhaps the first engineer I've met on a car launch who doesn't once mention the word 'compromise'. 'We are very happy with PASM,' he continues. 'It is absolutely the right thing for the GT3. It makes it faster, as you will see...'

Preuninger goes on to explain that Porsche looked long and hard at systems like BMW's SMG paddle-shift. 'It's great fun – sometimes – but it is not fast. If you want to go fast you must use your left leg. We tested these systems back-to-back with our manual 'box and it is definitely faster. And it gives you more options.' Even for drivers of average ability? Preuninger smirks: 'We don't build the GT3 for bad drivers.'

However, a DSG-style 'box is another story. 'Well, you must remember we invented the system (the PDK – Porsche Doppelkupplung – was first developed for the 956 Group C

car) and Mr Röhrl had it on his Pikes Peak Audi quattro back in 1987. It is very good, very fast, and handling our level of torque isn't a problem.' Preuninger, shadowed by the PR men, won't commit to it appearing on a Porsche any time soon, but smiles when he says 'we'll see'.

And the GT3RS? 'Yes, I am allowed to say it will happen, but nothing more.' He can't resist a few details, though. 'Look to the old GT3RS and you'll see similar differences.' Will it keep PASM (there's a rumour among customers that it will be ditched)? 'I can't say, but PASM is very good.'

Preuninger will happily talk for hours about the GT3, but most of all he's keen for us to drive the car. As he leaves the room, his sign-off is simply, 'You won't be disappointed.' He's not wrong.

disciplines, namely inconsistently bumpy roads and conversely smooth, grippy racetracks. In its standard setting the new GT3 is still very firm, but it feels more compliant and more composed than its predecessor (or even the conventional 'Sports' suspended Carrera/S), and that allows you to carry simply massive speed on the sort of roads that previously would have been the GT3 driver's worst nightmare.

On tight, narrow and dusty roads in the hills around Verona, the GT3 simply flows. And grips. The new Michelin Pilot Sport Cup tyres provide massive adhesion, as much as 1.4g in the dry. Porsche claims they even work better than a conventional tyre in the wet too, and by the look of the deep grooves on the inside half of the tread pattern there's no reason to doubt it. The Pirelli tyres, still not quite signed-off at the time of the press launch, are said to be even more extreme.

But, as Preuninger suggested, it's not the sheer grip and composure of the GT3 that defines its character. You'll be dazzled by the speed, of course; but it's the way the GT3 still engages and demands your concentration that is truly spellbinding. As you up the pace, the steering starts to come alive, and the front end starts that dance that has been integral to the 911 experience since year dot.

Use the endless and instantly available grunt to smear the massive 305-section rear tyres into the tarmac and the nose gently lightens, the car hunkered down and driving hard into the tarmac, steering jinking and shifting its weight subtly. The gearshift starts to function better the harder you work it too, allowing incredibly quick changes and meaning you can keep that engine continually in the sweet spot.

And when you do, the intensity of the noise and acceleration is epic. Some exhaust notes feel forced, tuned by a marketing department – the GT3's rich yowl is pure, functional and steeped in motorsport breeding. The engine is the heart and soul of the GT3, and when it's beating at 8000bpm you know you're in the presence of greatness.

These roads aren't ideal to really stretch the GT3's legs, but the traction control shows remarkable restraint even on sections that are obviously link roads between farmland for filthy tractors. Hit the Sport button (just next to the PASM mode button on the centre console) and the TC relaxes its tolerant grip further and you can even provoke useful slides without fear of stepping that millimetre too far on the loud pedal (usefully, Sport also changes the engine mapping, giving you an extra 11lb ft between 3000 and 4250rpm).

New GT3's nose is dominated by scoops that draw in cooling air for rads (it exits through the vent just ahead of the bonnet). Vent also stops unwanted cushion of air building up beneath car

'No waste,
no fuss; just pinpoint accuracy
and startling pace'

The traction control won't save you should you misjudge you turn-in speed and push beyond the limits of the front tyres (PSM, the stability control system, was considered too intrusive for the GT3), and like all 911s the GT3 tends to understeer gently when you're teasing its limits. But you can kill it with a lift as you turn in, and such is the rear grip that it's rare you'll actually tip the car into a big slide. Most of the time the GT3 simply feels keyed-in to the surface and wonderfully neutral.

It seems wise to wait for our allocated laps of the tight and technical Adria circuit to drive without TC's watchful eye. Adria's nearly 200km south of the designated road route, a good chance to sample the GT3 on the autostrada. Unfortunately, due to the tight time schedule, there's not much time to enjoy the effortlessly muscular cruising ability. Instead we just nail it through the smog of diesel fumes that seem to cling to every Italian main artery, running as close to flat-out as we dare.

At, erm, high speeds the GT3 feels rock solid. The front splitter, gaping air intakes and distinctive air outlet at the front on the bonnet, combined with an almost entirely flat underbody and a rear wing adorned with gurney flaps on its lower level create a very even aerodynamic load. And although Porsche claims only mild downforce, the GT3 feels pinned to the surface.

It's only lunchtime, but already I'm pretty sure the GT3 ticks all the boxes. It feels as sharp and focused as the celebrated 996 GT3RS, but virtually as useable as a standard Carrera. The outgoing GT3RS perhaps still holds the greater challenge, its writhing, tarmac-grazing ride making it the 911-

masochist's choice. Time will tell, but right now I've got a pressing engagement with an empty circuit…

With the PASM locked in its most extreme setting, the GT3 feels wonderfully adept out on the track. There's an economy about how it attacks the corners – the awesome stopping power bleeding into strong, responsive turn-in, mid-corner poise and then mind-scrambling traction. No waste, no fuss; just pinpoint accuracy and startling pace.

The optional PCCB brakes are simply stunning, and when you really get into the middle pedal the GT3 remains unerringly stable. As your confidence grows, that understeer is still evident, but it hardly tempers your pace and you quickly learn to drive around it. Through the one semi-quick corner (a blind left-hander) you can pitch the GT3 in on a trailing throttle, feeling the rear of the car steer the nose into the apex as you do. Then simply pick up the throttle, reduce your steering angle and drift out onto the exit kerb. Fantastic.

Of course, if the ultimate balance isn't quite to your liking there's huge scope for adjustment. GT3 owners can tweak everything from camber to ride height to anti-roll bar set-up. But when Walter Röhrl is charged with signing-off the final factory suspension settings you have to wonder if there's really much more for the GT3 to give.

Me? I think I'd leave it as it is. The GT3 has enough ability and adjustability to entertain and educate for years to come. It's madly fast and wickedly accomplished, but still lets you in on the fun even when you're not pushing at ten tenths. It may be a tad more civilised than its predecessor, but the new GT3 is still the 911 of choice.

SPECIFICATION

PORSCHE 997 GT3

■ **Engine**	Horizontally opposed 6-cylinder
■ **Location**	Rear, longitudinal
■ **Displacement**	3600cc
■ **Cylinder block**	Aluminium alloy, dry sump
■ **Cylinder head**	Aluminium alloy, dohc per bank, four valves per cylinder, VarioCam variable valve timing
■ **Fuel and ignition**	DME engine management, sequential multipoint injection
■ **Max power**	409bhp @ 7600rpm
■ **Max torque**	298lb ft @ 5500rpm
■ **Transmission**	Six-speed manual, rear-wheel drive, limited slip differential, TC
■ **Front suspension**	MacPherson struts, coil springs, gas dampers, PASM, anti-roll bar
■ **Rear suspension**	Multi-link, coil springs, gas dampers, PASM, anti-roll bar
■ **Brakes**	Ventilated discs, 350mm dia front, 340mm rear (PCCB optional), ABS
■ **Wheels**	8.5 x 19in front, 12 x 19in rear
■ **Tyres**	235/35x19 front, 305/30x19 rear, Michelin Pilot Sport Cup
■ **Weight (kerb)**	1395kg
■ **Power-to-weight**	298bhp/ton
■ **0-62mph**	4.3sec (claimed)
■ **Top speed**	192mph (claimed)
■ **Basic price**	£79,540

evo RATING ★★★★★

PORSCHE
935

Porsche flexed the regulations to breaking point with the 935, and in doing so created one of the most outrageous and spectacular sportscars ever

Words Roger Green | **Pictures** Andy Morgan

In the mid-Seventies the sportscar racing scene was in the doldrums. With an oil crisis still fresh in people's minds and the threat of global economic doom never far from the surface, manufacturer participation was on the wane. Immediate action was required, and the FIA's solution was a new set of rules that would offer teams the chance to bring more road-car relevance back to the championship through the Group 5 modified production class.

Porsche's chief engineer, Norbert Singer, took a very loose interpretation of those rules and designed a sportscar that would maximise the marque's chances of success at Le Mans and in the 1976 World Manufacturers' Championship. In doing so he created an icon, an extreme racing car with shocking performance and almost cartoon-like proportions.

Those regulations stipulated that the racers maintained only a vaguely similar frontal silhouette to the road car on which they were based – the Carrera RSR in this case – and Singer had the audacity and shrewd creativity to exploit the regs ruthlessly. In fact the 935 was so radical that even Porsche worried that the flat nose might be a step too far for the rule-makers and built a more conventional front end just in case the repositioned ground-hugging lights and louvered wheelarches were deemed too much. They weren't and neither were the crazy rear wheelarches that housed not only the enormous 15in-wide slick tyres but also included huge airboxes to feed the 2856cc flat-six motor along with its colossal single KKK turbocharger.

Together they created a swept volume of 3999cc, thereby just creeping under the 4-litre limit, and with cockpit-adjustable boost (between 1.2 and 1.5bar) the engine delivered a thumping 550-650bhp in the most spectacular

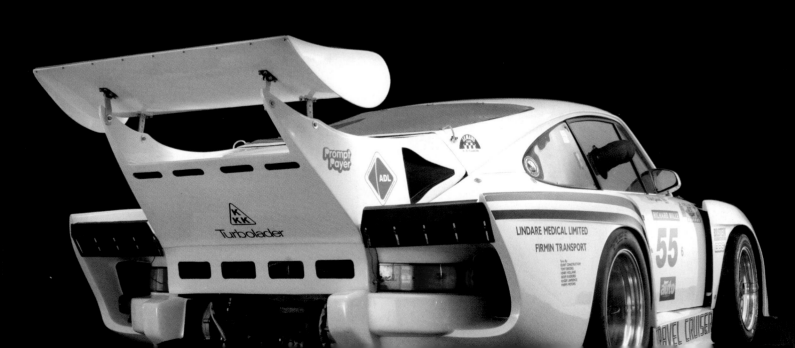

way possible. Turbocharging was still in its infancy, controlled only mechanically by the fuel injection system, so at low revs pressure built slowly, giving the drivers a tricky throttle-response issue. In an instant, nothing became everything, inducing wheelspin, oversteer, monumental acceleration and – if you backed off – a huge flare of flame from the tailpipes.

Spectators loved it, but it was a beast of a machine to drive, even for professional drivers of the era who came to the 935 following successful years in cars such as the 917 and the Ferrari 512.

Five-times Le Mans winner Derek Bell can't help but laugh when he recalls the sensation of driving a 935. 'The power was brutal like nothing else,' he tells us. 'You sat in this thing that resembled a 911, but in reality was nothing like one. It had this huge four-speed gear

lever that looked like a piece of scaffolding and you'd grab it and say "today it's you or me". It had raw, uninhibited power that felt like it was about to rip the transmission apart but never did. I just loved its exuberance. It would understeer as you turned in, all that power pushing the front tyres wide at first, but you'd stay on the throttle and wait as rear grip was overcome as the turbo kicked in. "Pitch it in and pray" was probably the best way to describe it. You'd drive like an animal – there was no point trying to be smooth and delicate, you took it by the scruff of the neck and just hung on to the steering wheel.'

Painted in the Martini Rossi colours, the two factory cars in the hands of Jochen Mass and Jackie Ickx gave the factory a winning start by taking the flag in the six-hour races at Mugello and Vallelunga in 1976, but from

'You sat in this thing that resembled a 911, but in reality was nothing like one'

This is one of the later developments of the 935, known as the K3 and raced by Kremer. It had two smaller KKK turbos in place of the original's single giant blower. Turbo lag was therefore reduced, but power was up – to 800bhp

'The 935 was so radical even Porsche thought

it might be a step too far for the rule-makers'

here on increasing competition from the BMW CSL squad made the title far from a foregone conclusion. In fact by the time they reached Le Mans the BMWs had taken three wins in a row. The French classic was a return to form, however, with the second factory car of Rolf Stommelen and Manfred Schurti the first Group 5 car home in 4th place overall, while a final win for Ickx and Mass eventually wrapped things up for Porsche at Dijon.

Despite cries of foul play, the following season saw the factory repeat its success with a twin-turbo version. By now there was also a small army of customer cars, so if the new, continually developing Martini cars failed to make the finish there was usually a customer team monopolising the top step of the podium. And then in 1978 came the craziest incarnation of all, 935/78 or, as it soon became known, Moby Dick.

Never one to miss a loophole, Singer was at the technical meeting where an agreement was made to allow the side panels to be cut (as exit points for the exhausts of the BMWs and other front-engine cars) and saw this as an opportunity to lower and lengthen the car, theoretically making it ideal for Le Mans. Moby Dick duly won first time out at Spa,

while at Le Mans with its new 950bhp engine it reached an incredible 227mph on the Mulsanne Straight and lapped nine seconds faster than the 935 of 1977. However, due to monumental fuel consumption (it had to pit every 35 minutes) and a small oil issue near the end of the race it only finished eighth. A 935 did win outright the following year, although it wasn't a factory entry but rather a Kremer-developed K3 version in the hands of Klaus Ludwig and Americans Bill and Don Whittington.

Further success in Europe and America continued until Group 5 was discontinued at the end of 1982 when Porsche created its next legend, the 956. In terms of audacity and explosive performance there was nothing like the 935. Derek Bell sums up the awe created by these cars perfectly: 'Power and the way it's delivered is what gives a car its character and it explains why these machines were so much more enjoyable to drive than the current LMP cars. For a driver, these things were the ultimate challenge, and if you were in one you knew you stood a good chance of winning. They never broke – at the end of the race there'd never even be a speck of oil in the engine bay.

'Porsche pushed the rules to their absolute limit but they knew how to get the job done.'

935/76

Layout	Rear engined, rear-wheel drive
Construction	Steel monocoque with glassfibre panels
Engine	Flat-six, turbocharged, air-cooled
Capacity	2856cc
Cylinder block	Aluminium alloy, dry-sumped
Cylinder head	Aluminium alloy, sohc per bank, two valves per cylinder
Fuel and ignition	Bosch mechanical fuel injection, single KKK turbocharger
Max power	630bhp @ 7900rpm
Max torque	434lb ft @ 5400rpm
Transmission	Four-speed manual, rear-wheel drive, locked diff
Front suspension	MacPherson struts, titanium springs, Bilstein dampers, adjustable anti-roll bar
Rear suspension	Trailing arms, titanium springs Bilstein dampers, adjustable arb
Brakes	Drilled and ventilated discs front and rear, 300mm diameter, four-piston calipers
Wheels	Front 16x10.5in, rear 19x15in alloys with Dunlop racing tyres
Steering	Rack and pinion, unassisted
Weight	970kg
Power-to-weight	660bhp/ton
0-60mph	3.3sec
Max speed	211mph

Many thanks to Peter Garrod for the loan of his K3.

The Turbo's back!

May 2006 saw the return of the all-weather supercar, with 472bhp and a new 4wd system ➲

New Turbo's 3.6-litre flat-six continues to employ twin turbos, but they now feature variable turbine geometry, a petrol-car first

've seen journalists at launches *run* from the transfer bus to bag a car. Most unseemly. No need today, though – there are maybe 20 new 911 Turbos in various colours gleaming in the Spanish sun; enough to go around. There's still a scrum around the PR man, though. I politely ask for a blue one as bids start flying in. 'Let's see… I've got a blue automatic,' he says. No thanks, I'll take a red manual. 'The auto is even quicker,' he says in a tone that suggests I won't be disappointed. No sale. Our names go down against the red six-speed.

A few miles after photographer Andy Morgan and I have loaded our gear into it and rumbled away, I'm wondering if the automatic might have been the better choice. Not because the Turbo is in any way lacking pace – it's got 472bhp, for goodness' sake – but because it feels, well, soft. Not soft in absolute terms, like a French car from the '60s, but in relation to other 911s. It's a subtle characteristic, but an unexpected one in a 193mph Porsche.

The press conference later will explain the various key features of the sixth-generation Turbo, including its variable turbo-blade geometry, active four-wheel-drive torque distribution and adaptive damping, so we don't yet know that the suspension feel can be changed at the prod of a button, but in its default setting the Turbo rides gently, its nose bobbing mildly

'The road spears straight for at least a mile. It's an irresistible invitation'

over bumps as if we've lashed all of Morgan's camera gear to the rear spoiler.

The feel of some of the controls adds to the sense that the Turbo has, in some way, been 'backed off' compared with other 911s. The gearshift isn't as mechanical and crisp as it could be, the clutch is light, the steering response a little damped. If this was, say, a Mercedes, it would be the most tactile and responsive I'd ever driven, but as a 911, and the most potent in the range at that, it seems a little too easygoing.

It's a deceptive car, though. We find ourselves sauntering along a new dual-carriageway, checking directions in the road book, when we pass a 120kph speed-limit sign. I glance at the speedo, sure that we're not far off that, and discover that we're cruising at over 160kph

(100mph). Yet there's barely a whisper of wind noise and the engine note is a murmur. Refinement is exceptional, then.

We crest a rise and, just as on the 993 Turbo launch over a decade ago (see page 117), the dark asphalt spears straight for the horizon for at least a mile. It's an irresistible invitation. The throttle hits its stop, and a moment later the boost floods in and the Turbo hammers forwards. It hauls sixth gear like most performance cars pull third, the electronic bar chart showing boost settled at around 0.9bar. We're told later that with the optional 'Sports Chrono' package, as fitted to this car, and with the appropriate mode engaged, the engine can deliver an extra 44lb ft on overboost for up to 10sec. Yet without troubling it we easily hit 275kph (170mph) before the next crest.

This is a seriously quick car, but I'm reminded of the ten-car 'ultimate 911' test we put together back in issue 36, which included the 996 Turbo. Its pace was undeniable, the ease with which it hit big speeds extraordinary, but compared with the more focused, normally aspirated models ranged against it, the Turbo didn't connect with or involve its driver to nearly the same degree. That said, the 996 was the most successful generation for the Turbo, with over 5500 units sold in its best year, its biggest market being the US. So why would Porsche change the formula?

On a curving feeder road that will take us to more-challenging rural roads, I give the throttle a squeeze and the twin-turbo flat-six growls as boost builds early. The fat rear tyres dig in and fire us around the loop, but when I ease off, the ➡

'The Turbo hauls sixth gear like most performance cars pull third'

tail seems to tuck back in. It's not tyre-slip but rather some lateral elasticity, as if the rear tyres have tall sidewalls with lots of give.

There's more to this new model, though, as we're about to discover. The small road we're now on has a pronounced crown and lolloping edges, and will soon present testing bends every couple of hundred metres. It's mostly third-gear stuff, and the Turbo is quickly into its stride, riding the bigger undulations calmly, taking the sting out of the more severe bumps and filling-in the hollows with aplomb. As the first proper corner rushes to meet us, I heft the wheel over and almost steer too hard into the turn as the previously floaty nose snaps to attention and digs-in instantly.

It's as if accuracy and immediacy were there all the time and it just needed a certain level of commitment to bring them out. The Turbo devours the next few miles in a very effective fashion, flowing along at a cracking rate, poised and precise. There's a momentary pause before the turbos deliver full boost, but you can factor it in by getting on the throttle a fraction earlier in the corners, assured that all that power will be

harnessed by the four-wheel-drive system.

The elements at work here are PSM (Porsche Stability Management), PASM (Porsche Active Suspension Management) and PTM (Porsche Traction Management). The first two we know from other 997s, where they very effectively control on-limit composure and adjust the damping to maintain poise. PTM is new and offers much greater control over torque distribution than the previous, viscous-coupling-based system. Working together with PSM and PASM, an electromagnetically controlled multi-plate clutch-pack divvies up the torque based on the input of a plethora of sensors to give active, optimum distribution (see 'Turbo tech', page 115).

The slightly disconnected feel of the Turbo can also be overcome by pressing the button depicting a damper. This firms up the suspension, transforming the Turbo in the process. Body control is notably tighter and the front end becomes much more alert, yet the car isn't at all nervous. The steering now feels more precise, its weight finely judged, and there's more feel through the simple, slim rim. The lateral give

in the rear suspension has gone, too. Put simply, you have more confidence because you feel so much better connected with what's going on at the wheels. Sure, the ride is a little harsher over rucked tarmac, but not uncomfortably so. I reckon this should be the default damper setting.

Specify the 'Sport Chrono' option (£1015) and you get another button beside the damper one. Marked 'Sport', it makes the same changes to the suspension but also facilitates overboost, engages a livelier engine-map and provides a 'primed' four-wheel-drive system that favours the rear 'for a more neutral stance', in the words of a senior Porsche engineer. Why Sport Chrono isn't standard on this near-£100,000 car isn't explained.

Press this button and the throttle becomes a little more sensitive, but I can't say that I detected any evidence of the overboost function. It should allow turbo pressure to increase by an additional 0.2bar, but the readout never strayed towards 1.2bar when I was looking. Thrust was dramatic, but consistently so.

After many miles location-hunting we finally find a corner that might suit some action shots. ❍

The teams gather in Red Square for the start. Top right: Stefan Preuss and his privately entered replica of a 1970s 911 Carrera Safari

We're not the first car to pass through the stage, which makes me feel a little better, but it still seems a bit, well, *lawless*, charging headlong down a forest track from which a local Lada driver had emerged, totally oblivious, only minutes before.

It's tight and twisty for the most part, and seriously slippery, but on the longer straights we're touching 80mph, crashing through potholes and deep standing water that conceals who knows what. Any one of these hazards could lead to a punctured tyre or, worse, deranged suspension. You just have to grit your teeth, ride your luck and keep your foot in.

And then from nowhere a logging truck appears right in front of us. I can squeeze through, but it's close. Seems the locals' idea of a closed stage is different to ours. By the time we emerge at the other end we're buzzing with adrenalin – and encouraged by the robustness of our Cayenne. It's the first time we've driven it in anger, there's more speed to come for sure, but best to keep something in reserve. After all, there's another 4000 miles to go…

A MOTORSPORT EVENT OF truly epic scale, the Transsyberia Rallye is a gruelling and at times perilous 4412-mile charge across the largest single landmass on Earth. Starting in Moscow and finishing some two weeks later in the Mongolian capital of Ulaanbataar, the Transsyberia's route is a combination of timed Special Stages separated by vast legs of road mileage designed to test driving and navigational skills, not to mention the outer limits of mechanical and human endurance.

Until recently the Transsyberia was a wholly amateur event contested by committed enthusiasts. Then in 2006 Porsche entered a pair of Cayennes, lightly modified and crewed by factory employees. They duly won outright, prompting the company to embark upon a much more serious programme for 2007 with the development of the Cayenne Transsyberia: a mildly but thoroughly modified Cayenne S built to tackle the hostile terrain of Siberia and Mongolia.

Sports exhaust apart, the Cayenne Transsyberia retains showroom-spec air-suspension and drivetrain – the familiar 385bhp 4.5-litre V8, coupled to a six-speed Tiptronic transmission – complete with a full complement of locking diffs and underbody protection plucked from the Cayenne

options list. A full roll-cage, racing seats, fire extinguisher and emergency GPS tracking and locating device provide peace of mind, while sturdy steel decking – onto which are strapped a pair of spare wheels, jerry cans, tool chests, an air-compressor, tents and a couple of rucksacks containing all our worldy belongings for the next fortnight – replace the rear seats. It's a long way from the kind of silhouette racers that steal the limelight on the Dakar, but it's unquestionably a proper piece of kit.

No less than 26 of the monsters have been built and entered, with Porsche having invited many of its worldwide importers to take part. Some of the larger territories, such as the USA, have entered three cars, while others, such as Porsche Cars Great Britain (for whom I am driving), have entered one. It's a massive effort, made all the more impressive by the driver line-up, which includes former three-time Paris-Dakar winner Rene Metge, multiple Pikes Peak winner and former hill record-holder Rod Millen and former WRC driver Armin Schwarz to name but three.

My team-mate – Neil Hopkinson – is a veteran off-road driver, having organised 4x4 tours through wilderness areas of Russia and the deserts of northern and central Africa for years, yet it's a mark of the challenge presented

'Touching 80mph at times, we crash through potholes'

by the Transsyberia Rallye that he, and all the competitors, from Metge to Meaden, are in awe of what's to come.

The rally starts in Red Square. It's a madly colourful place, and a million miles from the grey, forbidding backdrop for displays of military might that were beamed into our living rooms during the tail end of the Cold War. That said, Lenin's tomb *is* a bit spooky. Even so it's hard not to chuckle at the irony of driving our rally-prepared Porsche Cayenne into Red Square and parking alongside two dozen others in the shadow of the Kremlin. Harder still to reconcile being greeted with open arms by the deputy mayor of Moscow, while back home 'Red Ken' wages war on SUVs and their profligate capitalist owners…

START CEREMONY OVER, the entire rally entry plunges back into the maelstrom of commuting Muscovites. Even with a police escort to block side-roads and intimidate oncoming traffic, we still spend hours stuck in the quagmire of metal, inhaling the kind of rich, heady, pre-catalytically converted exhaust fumes I last smelled in the 1970s. My head bangs with the pollution.

Amidst the circus-like atmosphere in Red Square it was easy to forget that we're in a rally, and will soon be facing that first Special Stage, in the pine forests that skirt the small town of Petuschki about 80 miles east of the Russian capital. Neil is so at-one with the array of GPS navigation equipment nailed to the dashboard that he should (and probably does) come with a Garmin part number. I, on the other hand, don't, but bravely volunteer to navigate anyway and actually begin to enjoy stringing our route together. Amazingly we are amongst the first crews to arrive at the start of the stage.

Neil and I have agreed to share driving and navigating duties, so when the time comes to don our crash helmets, I'm in the hot seat. It's funny how the pressure of competition weighs on your mind. Ordinarily, the prospect of a 21-mile-long, sandy, muddy, up-and-down forest track and a Cayenne S to play with would have

me wearing a massive grin. But with the clock ticking and the responsibility of a) not crashing into a tree, and b) not being embarrassingly slow, I'm frowning with nerves. Twenty one miles later we emerge unscathed and on a high. What's abundantly clear is there's a delicate balance to be struck between pace and preserving the car.

After an overnight stop in Vladimir there's a longer road section and another Special Stage to face. It's another forest stage, but there are rumours of a deep water-hole, and with recent heavy rains there's a good chance it has become impassable. Trouble is, we won't know for sure until the first car attempts it.

As predicted, the water-hole is a monster, and there's a bit of a jam as half a dozen Cayennes form a disorderly queue. Eventually our turn comes to cross the turbid waters, but the Cayenne ahead is almost completely sunk, the hapless crew having clambered out onto the roof. Once it's been towed clear, we plunge in.

The bow wave comes clean over the bonnet, water rising up the side windows, but thanks to our snorkel the big V8 keep hauling, and with each wheel digging and clambering over submerged tree trunks, we emerge to complete the stage in 9th position.

With the cancellation of the next Special Stage, all that remains of the Russian leg is a hellish 2000-mile slog to complete in four days if we're to make our allotted appointment at the Mongolian border. To miss it would be a disaster, so we grit our teeth and adopt the local driving style: pretty much as fast as your vehicle will travel. We see some amazing sights, including the vast River Volga, the Ural mountains and the cities of Tjumen (Russia's oil capital) and Novosibirsk (the capital of Siberia), which confirm that though Russia has immense wealth and is developing at a dizzying pace, it will take generations for the farther-flung regions to prosper and erase that most characteristic landmark of Communism, the vast concrete tower block. We also get stopped repeatedly by the police and pay so many fines (Porsche-driving foreigners are clearly easy pickings for the copskis) we lose count. After two days we don't even bother to stop…

By the time we reach the Mongolian border most of us are utterly fatigued. Despite all our paperwork being in order, and completed months before we were due to arrive, crossing

from Siberia to Mongolia is a protracted process. Hours pass and nothing happens, until fellow driver Christian Pfeil-Schneider from the Colombian Arrow team acts as intermediary, remaining at the Siberian border post while groups of us are processed. If it weren't for him, we'd still be there now.

If you've watched Ewan McGregor and Charlie's Boorman's *Long Way Round* you'll think you have some idea what Mongolia is like. Believe me, you don't. Bad though they are, at least Russian and Siberian roads are, for the most part, surfaced. In Mongolia the gravel starts as soon as you drive into the no-man's land that separates it from Siberia. It's a jaw-dropping realm of huge skies, endless green mountains and a few spidery white tracks leading to the horizon. No tarmac. No road signs. No telegraph poles or pylons. No permanent buildings. Nothing. You feel like Charlton Heston in the opening minutes of *Planet of the Apes*. Except without the apes.

We've got six days to cover 1600 miles. Nothing after the endlessness of Russia, yet within just 40 miles one of the Italian crews suffers two punctures. They're not alone either, as we discover on arrival at our overnight halt in Olgy, the first major settlement in Mongolia. The scale of the country is humbling, the cleansing sense of purity and solitude uplifting after a week or more of chaotic Russian cities.

That night Mother Nature reminds us of our insignificance and vulnerability. We're all camped and fast asleep in a vast, rock-strewn valley – not ideal terrain for tent pegs – when the storm hits. It must be around midnight, and at first the novelty of being huddled in a tent while the wind howls outside is exciting. Then my tent repeatedly lifts clear of the ground and the screaming wind and subsequent storm awaken some primeval sense of fear deep within me. I spread-eagle myself across the tent floor as best I can, but there's little I can do except think happy thoughts and pray I'm not blown away.

Next morning I crawl out at first light (unheard of for me) to face another fear: the latrine. We've buddied-up with the Australian team of Paul Watson and journalist Dave Morley, who are typically sound blokes. They are also merciless piss-takers, especially when it comes to my aversion to sleeping under canvas and crapping in a hole. Suffice to say, morning ablutions Transsyberia-style are pretty unsavoury, and include sights (and sounds) I'll take to the grave.

Our first Special Stage in Mongolia is an absolute monster. Where we'd been doing 20 or 30 miles in Russia, here we're competing over stages hundreds of miles long, through completely uncharted terrain. And what terrain it is. The rudimentary roads can shred tyres in an instant, while bogs, rivers, boulders and gullies lie in wait at every turn. I'm driving again, which I'm relieved about, as navigation is crucial in this primordial wilderness.

What ensues has to be one of the most incredible, enjoyable, perilous and bewildering couple of hours' driving I've ever done. The poor Cayenne feels like it's being attacked by a mob wielding sledgehammers as we crash from one rock and gully to the next. We get a

Left: Porsche technicians disable the transmission on Meaden's damaged Cayenne so it can be towed to the next stop for repairs

The 997 GT2 is the fastest production 911 ever, but is it the ultimate Porsche? With competition like the GT3 RS, 993 GT2 and Carrera GT, it's got its work cut out...

Words **Jethro Bovingdon**

Pictures **Andy Morgan / Barry Hayden**

There's something strange going on here. I've just arrived in Yorkshire in the fastest 911 ever officially sanctioned by Porsche, yet suddenly it doesn't seem like a very special car at all. To my left there's an orange GT3 RS, huge carbon wing and minimal ride-height making it look like it's just escaped from an endurance race. Dead ahead, low and wide and buzzing to the fast idle of its bespoke 5.7-litre V10 sits a Carrera GT. And to rub salt into the wound, just behind the carbonfibre supercar I can make out the wacky-racer silhouette of the maddest 911 ever: the original Widowmaker, the 993 GT2. Its preposterous riveted arches, full to bursting point with Michelin's finest, make the gently swollen metalwork of the 997 GT2 I've driven here in look vaguely apologetic. If this was a test of pure charisma, the new GT2 might as

well just turn around and go home now.

It's a daunting line-up, for sure, richly talented and possessing a fascinatingly dangerous quality. However, on paper at least, the new GT2 should have each and every one of these icons covered. Porsche claims it's every bit as fast as the mid-engined, money-no-object Carrera GT, and more exploitable to boot, which means the GT3 RS (our favourite of the current 911 range and to many of our minds the most thrilling car we've ever driven) should be easy meat, and the 993 GT2 a relic that will dissolve under the intense pressure of the new GT2's 523bhp and 204mph potential.

However, speed and grip are just two of the measures that make a truly great car, and the GT3 RS and older GT2 bring other qualities to the party. The RS, for example, is a masterclass in pared-back precision. It's alive with feedback and is always right at the top of its game, ready to react to any and every input. Its purity of purpose is simply breathtaking. Can the heavier and turbocharged 997 GT2 replicate such a single-minded focus and

efficiency of execution? Perhaps, but by doing so will the harum-scarum GT2 spirit be lost?

A stark and probably terrifying reminder of that GT2 black magic, the original 430bhp 993 GT2 is here simply to see if the new car is true to its roots. The 997 GT2 should be fearsome. It should have an edge as sharp as a guillotine – anything less and the badge will sit uncomfortably on its tail. If the new GT2 can combine the speed of the Carrera GT, the purity of the RS and the sinister character of the old, air-cooled GT2 then it'll be a very special car indeed.

So let's take a close look at the 997 GT2, for it really does deserve some attention. With 523bhp and 501lb ft, it's the most powerful 911 road car ever produced (OK, so the wild GT1 had 544bhp, but I'd argue it wasn't really a 911 at all), and at 1440kg it's just 65kg heavier than the GT3 RS and a whopping 145kg less than the Turbo. Porsche claims it'll run to 204mph and hit 62mph in 3.7sec along the way, thanks in part to its launch control system. It's pretty handy around the corners too, and has posted

'The 997 GT2 should be fearsome. It should have an edge as sharp as a guillotine'

a 7min 32sec lap around the Nürburgring Nordschleife – a match for the 604bhp 1380kg Carrera GT. Whether the GT2 Walter Röhrl used was set up like this one is impossible to tell – everything from roll bars to ride height and camber can be adjusted – but clearly it's a devastating device for circuit work.

Of course, the GT2's defining feature is that all that big-turbo power is channelled through just the rear wheels, unlike the softer and more user-friendly four-wheel-drive 911 Turbo. Of more concern is that because the GT2 has bigger variable-vane turbochargers than the Turbo, the torque arrives much more violently. Once you're locked into the upright

carbon-shelled seats and have instinctively pulled the three-spoke steering wheel close, you glance left and down and two buttons immediately alleviate some of your fears – one says 'SC OFF', the other 'SC+TC OFF'. Which must mean the default mode is SC+TC on. This two-stage stability- and traction-control system is a first for a GT2, and although the masochists amongst you may bemoan the fitment of driver aids, I'm comforted to know that the hand of Röhrl is there to guide me at the limit. And you can still switch it off if you think Walter has always lacked a bit of commitment. Me? I'll leave it on just for the moment, thanks.

Inside, it's business as usual, which means function over form. There's nothing of the drama of an F430 or Gallardo here, but £131,000 does buy you a sense of incredible integrity. It's not just the materials, it's the feeling that zings back through the suede-rimmed steering wheel, the way you can sense the suspension working hard yet feel the structure itself refusing to wobble or flex. Everything that requires an input has an engineered exactness.

The gearshift is heavy and awkward when cold and still requires effort and thought even when thoroughly warmed through, every shift a reminder that the GT2 is a wickedly potent car. Paddling around below the point where the turbos really start to spin, the flat-six's soundtrack is deep and thick, the gentle sighs of the turbochargers' plumbing giving the GT2 an extreme character. Even before it's lit-up, this car feels almost like a product of one of the many Porsche tuning outfits.

Compared with the 997 Turbo, the GT2 suffers from considerable lag, but in reality the power band is plenty wide enough – peak torque is available from 2200 to 4500rpm, although it seems things really get going at 2800rpm and from there it just takes off and hurtles into the limiter at 6750rpm. The delivery is surreal. The way the car launches as the turbos spin-up is shocking, but the real trick is that this hammer-blow isn't just maintained but actually builds into something even fiercer as the revs climb. Over 5500rpm the digital boost display coolly reads '1.4 bar' and anything short of a Carrera GT is a rapidly diminishing irrelevance. This thing is senior-league supercar fast, no question.

You need to hang on to it, too. The huge torque and stiff set-up make the GT2 feel like it's tying itself in knots. It skips from bump to bump, rear wheels grabbing for traction, power multiplying, speed building at a demented rate. It's rampant and intense and requires every fibre of skill you can muster to control. In the face of this onslaught, the first few minutes of exposure to the GT2 are simply mind-scrambling. Yorkshire is renowned for its fast, ragged tarmac and up here on the moors the GT2 feels every inch the sort of car of which legends are made. Lose concentration for an instant and the GT2 will swallow you whole, bones and all.

I don't mind admitting that I'm genuinely shocked by the GT2's furious pace. It's as though Porsche has grown tired of manufacturers like Audi and Nissan grabbing the limelight and has thrown everything at making the GT2 as ferocious as possible. Mission accomplished. The GT2 is as outrageous a car as I've driven. Ever. I never thought I'd be climbing into a 993 GT2 just for a bit of respite…

THE SKIES ABOVE ARE textured like a granite cliff-face, but thankfully any moisture is locked in. Short bursts of sunshine have dried the roads but the temperature is low and all of these cars deserve a healthy dose of respect in such conditions. Not least the only car here with no traction control at all: the 993 GT2. The air-cooled GT2 is for many people the last

Right: hairy 993 GT2 from the late '90s (the blue car) is the benchmark we'll use to see if the new GT2 – fitted with traction and stability controls for the first time – has gone soft

993 GT2

Engine	Flat-six, twin-turbo
Location	Rear, longitudinal
Displacement	3600cc
Cylinder block	Aluminium alloy
Cylinder head	Aluminium alloy, sohc per bank, 2v per cylinder
Fuel and ignition	Electronic engine management and fuel injection
Max power	430bhp @ 5750rpm
Max torque	395lb ft @ 4500rpm
Transmission	Six-speed manual, rear-wheel drive, limited-slip differential
Front suspension	MacPherson struts, coil springs, dampers, anti-roll bar
Rear suspension	Multi-link, coil springs, dampers, anti-roll bar
Brakes	Cross-drilled and vented discs, 322mm front and rear, ABS
Wheels	9.0 x 18in front, 11 x 18in rear, aluminium alloy
Tyres	235/40 ZR18 front, 285/35 ZR18 rear, Michelin
Weight (kerb)	1290kg
Power-to-weight	339bhp/ton
0-62mph	4.0sec (claimed)
Max speed	184mph (claimed)
Price	£135,000 (1995)
On sale	1994-99

evo RATING ★★★★★

'The GT is a feast of gorgeous engineering'

Left: lightweight wood gearknob – echoing that of the 917 racer – typical of the Carrera GT's enthralling attention to detail

torquey and so smooth that it makes for effortless progress, the beautiful gearbox is quick and intuitive, the brakes and accelerator perfectly weighted. The steering is smooth and light too, and is nothing like as distracted by surface changes as a 911 helm, yet still the quality of feedback is rich and dense and the front-end reacts to the tiniest input with startling immediacy. There's no slack at all – the car responds with total obedience and without a millisecond's delay.

The long wheelbase, wide track and mid-mounted engine mean the GT is much more stable than the 911s on the rutted Yorkshire roads. It's stiff, certainly, but not as unforgiving as a GT3 RS or GT2, and the wheels never leave the ground. Turning around in a steep lay-by for photography reveals wheel travel is tiny (a front wheel pops into the air as the rear reverses down the steep slope) but you'd never guess as much – it breathes with the road.

It's mightily quick too, lacking the GT2's thuggish mid-range thump but countering with an incredibly cultured delivery that soars past 8000rpm with a singular, piercing howl. At the top end it's still a chunk faster than the GT2, but finding the room to use the last 2000rpm is something of a challenge. Finding the bravery to use it is even harder, because the Carrera GT is a highly strung device and such is its precision and potential that it feels considerably more intimidating than even the hardcore GT2.

That sounds crazy when you think that the GT2 has turbo-lag and is rear-engined, but the mid-engined, normally aspirated Carrera GT feels set up to work only within its sky-high limits – what lies beyond is almost impossible to deliberately access on the road and almost certainly requires superhuman skill to exploit even on the track. The GT has no stability control and its traction control is best described as 'tolerant' – you can easily spin a GT without the electronics waking up at all. So

'The new GT2 can't compete with the glamour of the pumped-up original'

'The RS feels like a perfectly balanced package'

it is an intimidating experience, but when you relax and settle in to that engine and a chassis that doesn't roll or squat or dive and yet still conveys tiny shifts in balance through your seat, a whole world of thrills opens out ahead of you. It's just so pure, so mechanical.

With the 911s it's all about getting the nose in and then using the traction, but the GT is much easier to turn-in. There's no understeer at all and no need to wait for the front to settle before pouring on the power. You turn and balance the chassis with power simultaneously. You can feel the huge grip, and so as each bend unfolds you can start to use more and more revs. Now you sense the car starting to really drive through a corner, maybe even the rear beginning to have a subtle steering influence.

Everything here is minutely balanced and you must be as accurate as the car to get the most from it. Start to nail the braking zones and gearshifts and you feel the way the GT grows in stature with every confident input. Suddenly you're immersed in one of the great driving experiences. The Carrera GT is all about sensations: the noise, the epic power, the solidity of the braking and unfiltered texture flowing back through the steering. Despite its

on-paper performance, the Carrera GT isn't the quickest car across the ground here, but it is a unique and all-consuming experience.

Roger Green, following in the 997 GT2, was well placed to judge the relative pace of the two cars: 'There isn't a lot in it, really. If I was caught off-boost, the Carrera GT instantly stole ten car lengths that the GT2 couldn't recover, but if we were both hooked-up, the GT2 isn't too far away in raw speed. It's quite easy to keep up actually – you can see just how much respect the Carrera GT demands. What a noise, though! I could hear it above the GT2's engine even when you pulled well ahead a couple of times.'

So far the new GT2 is ticking all the boxes. It's near-as-dammit as fast as the Carrera GT and just as scary as the old 993 GT2. Once the shock of the performance has worn off, the challenge remains, and as you get familiar with its chassis you can feel the deep-seated quality. The PASM damping is exceptional in its standard mode, traction is simply phenomenal and all the classic 911 traits – superb steering, immense braking and that sense that the car is alive underneath you – are intact. Getting the nose turned-in, releasing the flood of torque

and feeling the front wheels unload as the rears dig into the surface is pure magic. If the aim was to build a GT3 RS with another 100bhp, then I reckon Porsche has just about pulled it off. It's the most exciting car I've driven for a very long time.

With purple and black slowly biting into the grey sky, I drive back to our overnight stop at the White Swan in Pickering full of admiration for the 997 GT2. I never thought it justifiable to spend £131,070 on a 911 when a plain GT3 is £80,660, but now I'm not so sure. It's faster than a 430 Scuderia, which costs £172,500, and it makes the £152,000 Gallardo Superleggera feel clunky. Maybe it's just too fast for the road, though. Maybe the GT3 RS is a better package. All will be revealed tomorrow…

PARKED SIDE-BY-SIDE, killer road draped lazily over the moors behind them, there's no question a bright orange GT3 RS is a more enticing prospect than a silver-grey GT2. It's not just the colour but the detail: the simple carbon wing, the jutting front splitter – the whole car looks like it's crouching in its starting blocks waiting for the pistol. Inside it's only subtly different to the GT2, but again the

N

ine five six. Of all the numbers that define Porsche's phenomenal record in motorsport, this one is arguably the most remarkable. It belongs to the car that did it all for Porsche when, after the FIA's radical re-writing of the World Endurance Championship rules in 1982, there was everything to do. It did it all for Derek Bell, too. 'What can I say about the car that set me up for life?' the five-times Le Mans winner told us when we spoke to him shortly after this studio shoot. Quite a lot, as it turned out.

Porsche had dominated international sportscar racing through the second half of the '70s but, at the end of the '81 season, the 935 and 936 that had been virtually untouchable in the Group 5 and Group 6 classes were rendered obsolete overnight by the new system of Group A, B and C classes. Groups A and B required a limited production run for eligibility but Group C was for prototypes regulated by

a set of dimensions and, more controversially, the amount of fuel that could be used per race, effectively capping the engine's performance potential.

Some manufacturers might have regarded this as a setback but Porsche, not untypically, saw it as an opportunity to pull further ahead of the opposition. The 956 was the first all-new Porsche racer in over a decade and, apart from sharing its turbocharged, aluminium flat-six engine, marked a dramatic departure from the 936, parts of which dated back to the late '60s.

It wasn't just the new aluminium monocoque, with its front and rear subframes, that set the 956 apart, since much of the competition had moved to a monocoque structure as well. What made the difference was Porsche's attention to detail, especially in aerodynamics. The rear coil-spring/damper units for the all-round double wishbone suspension, for instance, were mounted on top of the gearbox to keep them out of the airflow. Where Porsche levered in

a rear advantage, though, was with ground effects. The new Group C cars would be allowed to have some ground effect but, to prevent this becoming extreme, the regulations stated that between the front and rear axles the bottom of each car should be completely flat. They didn't stipulate what should happen behind that. So Porsche fitted the 956 with large venturis (air tunnels) starting just behind the mandatory flat section and angled steeply back through the tail as they passed alongside the slightly upwardly-tilted flat-six engine and five-speed gearbox. In conjunction with the simple but effective Kevlar-reinforced plastic body, the 956 generated over three times more downforce than the 917, making it the first true ground-effects Porsche.

The 956 was designed and built by Porsche System at Zuffenhausen under the guidance of Norbert Singer. To improve fuel consumption, its 2649cc flat-six engine ran smaller turbos than in the '81 936, with the boost set at a relatively modest 1.1 bar, but it still developed 620bhp in race trim. From the outset, the objective was to win Le Mans but it was agreed that 1982 was to be a development year for the car. Derek Bell recalls the first race, the Six Hours at Silverstone: 'Everyone asks if it was a job coming to terms with ground effect, and I have to say I didn't really notice it unduly. You gradually went faster and faster. And then you stopped and someone else drove for an hour and so on. I think the fact we were doing a shakedown – just five laps and in – meant we never got round to feeling tired.

'But the car itself was just phenomenal. When we went to that first race in May at Silverstone, Jackie (Ickx) went out and did a 1:15.3 or something, which put us on pole, about a second ahead of the Group 6 Lancias. And then, on race morning, [director of racing] Peter Falk came up to me and said "you are not going to win the race". And this coming from Porsche – usually so quietly confident. I asked what he meant, and he said "well, we didn't calculate on the fuel".

'Jackie had never done a fuel stint before. Nor had I. So he went out and did the first hour and then came in and Falk said to me, 'Derek, you'll have to start lapping in 1:21s or you'll run out of fuel'. So I'm cruising round Silverstone in fifth gear and downshifting for the chicane and Becketts, just to try and salvage a position at all. It was the most desperate way to go racing and I was very outspoken afterwards. It was never really written that Porsche had made "a bit of an error", only that it used the race to "calibrate fuel consumption". And, of course, they soon got it right. But, at that point, it was a major cock-up. With hindsight, of course, it was an outstanding FIA regulation. It helped cause one of the very rare spin-offs from motor racing that goes into road cars. It improved fuel consumption by 20 per cent. Instead of 4mpg we got 5.'

After that early mistake and defeat by the quick but frequently unreliable Lancias, the 956, Ickx and Bell hardly ever looked back. In the following four years, the 956 notched up four consecutive outright victories at the Le Mans 24 Hours and dominated international sportscar racing. As well as speed and reliability, the 956 also had numbers on its side. A total of ten works cars was supplemented by no fewer than 16 sold to private teams.

The IMSA GTP championship in the USA was also a natural battleground for the 956, being all but identical to Group C.

'The team notched up four consecutive outright victories at Le Mans'

Cockpit basic and (in heat of battle) absolutely roasting. Centre: venturi created 'ground effect'. Below: Mass and Bellof raced this car at '83 Le Mans; led for first four hours, lying second when holed piston ended race

J. MASS
S. BELLOF

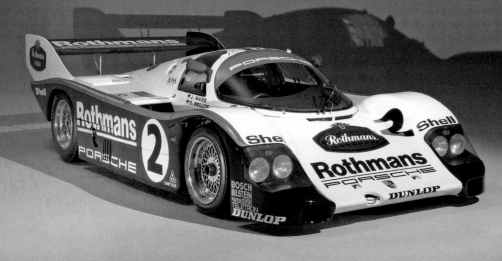

'It was the most
fantastic car
to attack with'

956 '008' had a
distinguished race
career, including
victory at the
Norisring with Bellof
in '83. Below: team-
mate Bell found 956
physical but hugely
rewarding to drive

Year zero, the spanner-strewn garage of a semi in the 'burbs. It's 1964. Lotus is a kit-car manufacturer erroneously claiming you can bolt together an Elan S2 between mugs of coffee over the course of a lazy weekend, Ferrari has won at Le Mans for the penultimate time and family motoring is a Vauxhall Victor. In the United States, Ford is tugging the wraps off its very first Mustang; in Italy, tractor maker Ferruccio Lamborghini has just built his first car.

But in Germany, Porsche is being threatened with legal action by Peugeot. A year earlier, the small, independent company founded in 1931 by Ferdinand Porsche decided to call its new car the 901. Peugeot, which insists it has already registered the numerical sequence as a model name, has different ideas. So the new Porsche is renamed 911.

A small, rear-engined car with an air-cooled powerplant – just like the VW Beetle-derived 356 it succeeds – the 911 has a drag coefficient of 0.381, disc brakes all round, and rack and pinion steering. Its dry-sump 1991cc flat-six engine develops 130bhp at 6100rpm and 128lb ft of torque at 4200rpm. It sounds like no other production engine in the world: hard, metallic, fast. And it is, with a 0-60mph time of 8.5sec and a top speed of 130mph.

Although no one knows it yet, the 911 is the future. Not just Porsche's, but the future into which every subsequent sports car is launched; a future influenced by the 911. Although its engine is theoretically in the worst place, it encapsulates the best idea anyone has ever had about travelling quickly on four wheels: what matters isn't speed but speed-to-size ratio. The sports car that takes up less road is the one that can use it to greater effect. It has more space, more options, more chances for fun. The Porsche 911 will never abandon this idea, even

Company founder Ferdinand Porsche on the Grossglockner Pass. The pass was the scenic route between home and the factory and also used for testing

Below: the pass winds its way high into the Austrian Alps, where snow covers the slopes even in summer and the air is tangibly thinner

THE ROAD

Getting to Porsche's roots in Gmünd, Austria, where the company started making its own cars in 1948, can take you on some terrific mountain roads. One such is the Grossglockner Pass, which is the more dramatic of the two main routes the Porsche family and its early test drivers used to get from the family estate at Zell am See to the converted sawmill at Gmünd.

Wolfgang Porsche, grandson of Ferdinand and today chairman of the Porsche supervisory board, well remembers the drive up the Glossglockner as a small boy sat next to his father, Ferry. The company continued to use it even after it had returned to its pre-war Stuttgart base.

Herbert Linge, who road-tested early 911s, also has fond memories of the pass. 'We did a lot of testing at night,' he recalls. 'I remember saying to myself, "This will be a very good car." That first impression is important. And the first test driver is the most important for any car, because his views set the direction for all that follow.'

One important early test was the 1965 Monte Carlo rally. The 911 had just been launched and PR boss Huschke von Hanstein thought it would be a good publicity stunt to enter one in the rally.

Peter Falk, who later ran Porsche's racing team, co-drove the 911 with Linge. 'It was the first ever motorsport competition for the 911,' he recalls. 'We'd homologated it the week before so we could enter. We came fifth overall.'

POWERING UP

A lightweight flat-six overhanging the rear wheels. That, and elements of the resultant exhaust note, is about all these cars have in common in engine terms. As originally configured, the 911 engine gave 130bhp at 6100rpm from its 1991cc. It was air-cooled in then-normal Porsche and Volkswagen fashion, a large fan dominating the engine bay, but engineer Ferdinand Piëch (Ferry Porsche's nephew and he of later VW Group overlordship) took the engine far away from any Beetle genes.

Ferry Porsche wanted the engine to be stretchable, maybe as far as 2.7 litres, but in the end it went as far as 3.6 (in the 964 and 993), without a fundamental redesign. As a 993 Turbo it made up to 430bhp; in a 935 race car, with four valves per cylinder and massive boost, it touched 800bhp.

Piëch's design involved a single overhead camshaft per bank, operating valves via rockers so they could be positioned optimally in a part-spherical combustion chamber. Each cylinder head straddled three finned cylinder barrels. Beneath the crankshaft was a gear-driven layshaft that would in turn drive the two camshaft chains. To help keep the centre of gravity low, there was no oil sump – oil was fed from a separate tank.

There were various fuelling systems over the years, the original triple-choke carburettors giving way first to pump-type injection, later to a continuous-spray system, before electronics arrived in the 1980s.

'Before we make our pelt for the clouds, we pause

though it will inevitably grow larger over the years.

As the 911 flick-book swells with each successive generation, the image will morph smoothly into the future. No other car will evolve with so little disruption to the visual flow. The sound, the minimalism, the peerless steering feel, the oversteer. All define the origin of the 911 species. All can be experienced in the very first 911.

In 1965, a Polo Red example, chassis number 300722, rolls off the production line in the southern Stuttgart suburb of Zuffenhausen. It has a black leather interior and a real timber dashboard. Its engine runs a compression ratio of 9.0:1 and is fed its fuel/air mixture by two temperamental triple-choke 40PI Solex carburettors, missing the point at which Porsche switches to more dependable twin Webers by just a few months. It travels to the warmer, kinder climes of the States where, in 1988, it's bought by part-time Florida resident and hardcore Porsche collector Otto 'Ottocar' Jacobs, who transports it back to his other home in Vienna, Austria. And there it stays, gathering miles slowly, waiting patiently for the call…

SHAPE SHIFTING

Originally styled by Ferry Porsche's oldest son, Ferdinand Alexander or 'Butzi', the 911 was a light, delicate, airy-looking creation at the start. It increased in machismo, wheelarch muscle and aerodynamic addenda over the years, but take away the rounded bumpers of a late-'80s/early-'90s 964 and it would still look much like our early car. Even the 993 kept the same door and window shapes and basic dashboard, and the roots were still clear in the rest of it.

Air-cooling makes for a light engine – useful when it's hanging out the back – but it's too noisy for modern legislation. It's also hard to get even cooling across all cylinders, and the higher running temperatures bring high nitrogen oxide emissions. It was inevitable that air-cooling would end, and the engine was radically redesigned with water-cooling, first appearing in the Boxster of 1996. Now the crankcase halves included conventional cylinder blocks and the heads got two camshafts each, directly actuating four valves per cylinder.

Thus the engine continued, growing to 3.8 litres for the Carrera S and gaining increasingly sophisticated variable valve timing – until now. The obvious change for the new engine is that it has direct fuel injection, allowing a higher compression ratio thanks to the cooling effect of injecting fuel at the top of the compression stroke, and greatly improving both fuel efficiency and emissions.

But there's more to the engine than new cylinder heads. Virtually every component is new, and there are 40 per cent fewer of them, making for a stiffer structure and a 5kg weight reduction. That layshaft is one obvious deletion – now the chains are driven directly from the crankshaft.

The Carrera S here has 380bhp – nearly three times the original 911's output from not quite twice the capacity. The 0-60mph time has halved yet real-world fuel consumption is about the same, possibly better. Ferry Porsche would be amazed. And to think that Porsche, in the late 1970s, wanted to kill off the 911 and its flat-six altogether…

in a parking area, get out and, frankly, just gawp'

All changed with the all-new 996 and its 997 evolution, which, with the Boxster, helped transform Porsche from a company in deep financial trouble to probably the most profitable car company in the world. That's because these cars are much cheaper and easier to build than the old generation, and because the front halves of Boxster and 911 are practically identical.

Today's car has grown, inevitably. Its shape is recognisably that conceived by Butzi Porsche, but it's 272mm longer, 198mm wider, 139mm longer in the wheelbase and 375kg heavier.

YEAR 44, THE *Guardian Weekend* supplement, June 20, 2008. There it is again. The iconic profile of the original 911, this one in a dark forest green. The double-page Porsche advert is entitled 'Purity of Purpose' and contains just a few lines of copy with a conspicuous subtext that, in essence, reads thus: half a lifetime has passed since we made this car, but the single-minded design purity at its heart lives on in the very latest 911, available from July 5.

The magazine is resting on the passenger seat of a glintingly new second-generation '997' Carrera S procured from Porsche's press garage a handful of days before its official UK release. And that passenger seat is rushing towards the Austrian town of Zell am See at a speed entirely compatible with the Porsche-endorsed German sensibility that keeps decent chunks of autobahn unrestricted: 'Freie Fahrt für frei Bürger'. Or 'Free driving for free citizens'. Or – for a few sublime seconds at least – roughly 190mph with a slight tail wind.

It seems only right the ad should be present at the testing of its proposition that the current edition of the world's most famous sports car shares more with its ancestor than just a profile

and a name. Over how great a time-span can coherence be stretched? Is Porsche's spirit perpetual, as indelible as the letters in a stick of rock? The answers are coming. As the latest Carrera S devours the distance between itself and the Austrian Alps, Otto's red 1965 911, conserving its energy on the back of a low loader, has left Vienna and is heading for the same place.

The timelines are scheduled to converge at noon, July 2, on the breathtaking Grossglockner Pass, which climbs high enough into the thinning air for the sky to turn a deeper shade of blue, and the cheeks of the cyclists slogging up the endless incline engulfed in clouds of diesel fumes belched out by tourist coaches to turn a whiter shade of pale. Legend has it that while testing an early 356 prototype on the Grossglockner for his father Ferdinand, the young Ferry Porsche nearly came to grief when the car's frame buckled, part collapsing the rear torsion-bar housing. Ferry, being the engineer he was, effected a running repair with two pieces of scrap iron from a friendly road worker nearby and continued on his way. At full speed.

There was less traffic then, of course. Today, Austria's highest and most spectacular

mountain pass attracts almost a million visitors a year and, as Otto and I queue up at the toll booths to hand over our 28 euros, it seems like most of them have decided to make their sojourn today. Still, these are Porsche 911s – we'll pass them on the straights. Between us we have 510bhp, after all.

But its distribution does seem a little one-sided. With 380bhp, the latest Carrera S has three times the power of the original 911. At 186mph, it's 56mph faster flat out and, equipped with the optional PDK dual-clutch transmission, it sprints from rest to 60mph in a few fractions over four seconds, virtually half the time. Yet while the original struggles to crack 20mpg and puffs out emissions you can actually see, the new car boasts 27.7mpg on the combined cycle and emits just 240g/km of CO_2, making it even greener than a mainstream coupe like Audi's TT V6. But while the distance between the two cars' technologies can only be calculated by astronomers, there's no doubt which is the better-looking car.

Before we make our pelt for the clouds, we pause in the broad expanse of parking area, get out and, frankly, just gawp. The juxtaposition of first and last isn't something you'd expect to see

Interior of the 1965 911 (above and right) has stood the test of time – its elegant simplicity is as appealing as ever and it still feels well screwed together. Dashboard of the 2008 car (top right) clearly influenced by that of the earliest 911s; note how the rev counter is still centre-stage amongst the dials. Right: seats in the 1960s car offer little in the way of lateral support; thankfully it's a different story with the modern items (far right)

'The Carrera S scythes through a series of manic ess-bends with astonishing speed and precision'

outside of a museum and the static comparison is too fascinating to hurry. The first impression is that the Carrera S, normally a paragon of space efficiency, seems fat and bloated and the original 911 dainty and cute. More than that, it makes the 997 look bland and somehow unresolved, like a lump of Plasticine that's been endlessly remodelled with no real sense of conclusion.

It's all down to Butzi – eldest son of Ferry Porsche, grandson of Ferdinand. As is sometimes the case with the genuinely gifted, the masterpiece gets done early and its true worth isn't appreciated for years. It's probably significant that style guru and appreciator of all things cool Sir Terence Conran loves the air-cooled original. One suspects Conran wasn't too bothered about the scattered switchgear. He liked the shape, the noise, the feel.

What happens next when I climb back into the precise embrace of the Carrera's exquisitely supportive seat, fire-up the 3.8-litre, direct injection flat six, nudge the chunky PDK

selector back to 'D' and accelerate into a rare patch of clear road is predictable. The image of Otto's pursuing red 911 in the rear view collapses to a dot in a matter of seconds. The Carrera S is fast in a way that the old timer can't even begin to comprehend.

Satisfaction flows almost immediately from the blinding potency of the engine, the smooth, quicksilver shifts of the PDK transmission and the sheer levels of grip served up by the chassis. As the road starts to climb more seriously towards turns three and four, the almost disdainful effortlessness of the direct injection motor's delivery is a genuine jaw-slackener, registered initially as a linear strain increase on your neck muscles, and then a sharper, exponential surge of pace as the VarioCam Plus valvegear starts to adjust the camshaft angle.

Now the curves are better sighted. A series of sweeping semi-hairpins blends into a section of manic ess-bends that the Carrera S scythes through with frankly astonishing speed and precision. It's extreme, but curiously clinical,

'With 380bhp, the latest Carrera S has three times the power of the original 911'

HOW LOW CAN YOU GO?

Here's the single most obvious evolution in the Porsche 911 look. Our early car was made with wheels just 4.5in wide, wearing 165 HR15 tyres with an almost balloonish look compared with today's ultra-low profile. A narrow tyre tread was more tolerant of camber changes in the suspension, but in fact Porsche would have liked to have used bigger tyres on the back than on the front because the rears had so much more work to do.

However, German legislation demanded that a spare wheel could be used on any corner, so different tyre sizes front and rear were ruled out until the Goodrich space-saver was officially approved as a temporary substitute for any wheel of the same rolling radius.

The Carrera RS 2.7 was the first 911 with rear wheels wider than the fronts (7in versus 6in), and the rear wheelarches flared out to suit. The tyres grew from there, with the final original-shape, pre-964-era Turbo wearing 245/45 ZR16s on 9in rims. Even that sounds tame compared with the new Carrera S, though, whose 11in-wide rear rims wear 295/30 ZR19 rubber. The fronts, meanwhile, are 235/35 ZR19 on 8in-wide rims.

'If the Carrera S were to look this good after 44 years, I'd be staggered'

lacking even the signature nose-bobbing over certain combinations of bumps that characterised the previous-generation 997's damping. The chassis's grunt/grip balance, kept in check so effectively by the PSM stability control, is a thing of unshakeable resolve up here in the mountains, but it's almost too easy, too prescribed by peak forces rather than genuine feel. So long as I stay out of the Sport setting – which stiffens the suspension and speeds the shifts still further but does nothing to sharpen the already eye-watering pace – it even rides reasonably. Braking demands a confident push on the pedal, but the vented steel discs are phenomenally powerful and seemingly tireless.

It takes literally minutes for Otto's 911 to catch up as I wait in one of the ascent's numerous car parks. Otto explains that the car's been running a little rich even at sea level. Up here in the thin air it's struggling to clear its throat. So rather than push on to still higher altitudes, we decide to turn around so that I can

drive it back down the pass.

The first shock is the driver's seat: low, squidgy-comfortable, dentist chair-style head-rests the size of rolled towels, zero lateral support. The second is the steering wheel: enormous, with a pencil-thin wooden rim and too close to my chest. And the third is the gearlever: a bent metal wand protruding from the floor with foot-long throws and a dog-leg shift pattern that places 1st out on a limb and digging about an inch into the seat cushion when it's adjusted for a short-arse like me. But, oh, the build quality. If the Carrera S were to look this good after 44 years, I'd be staggered. And the noise. Porsche has cleverly contrived to make the water-cooled 911s sound as magical as their air-cooled antecedents. In isolation, you'd almost believe it had managed it, but it hasn't.

The real thing has more metallic edge, more harmonic richness, more exhilaration and excitement. And while it's true that the PDK transmission changes gear at least 100 times

BRAKING POINT

The 911 had disc brakes all round right from the start, with ventilated discs – all round, again – appearing first on the 911S in 1966. They got ever larger and more powerful over the years, those on the 3.3-litre 911 Turbo (or 930) of 1978 being borrowed from the flat-12-engined 917 racing car, complete with drilled discs. There was no brake servo on the first 911s, and not until 1977 did every 911 variant have one.

Today's Carrera S has rather larger brakes than the original 911, front disc diameter having risen from 282 to 330mm, rears from 290 to 330mm. More significant is the increase in disc thickness – the fronts are now a hefty 34mm – and the greater brake-pad area, calling for four-piston calipers. The optional carbon-ceramic brakes have yet bigger calipers.

Nowadays the brakes play a part in the stability systems, being applied independently and automatically as required, but what hasn't changed is the fact that a 911's rear brakes contribute a higher proportion of the total stopping effort than those of most other cars. The heavy tail is why. Early 911s had a pressure-limiting valve to stop the lightly laden front wheels locking up under heavy braking. Electronics do the job now.

EU 54 ZZ

Right: second-generation 997 Carrera S may be able to leave the 1965 911 for dead, but that doesn't make it the most entertaining of the pair to drive

STRUT STUFF

The Beetle had torsion bars. So why shouldn't a 911? Unlike the Beetle and its Porsche 356 descendant, though, the original 911 used MacPherson struts (above left) and lower wishbones at the front to maximise boot space in the nose, with the lack of the struts' usual coil springs maximising the space benefit. Semi-trailing arms located the rear wheels, their reduced camber change compared with Porsche's former swing axles giving rather more stable handling.

The 964 changed to coil springs, not least to allow the front wishbones some longitudinal compliance hard to achieve when they are solidly anchored to longitudinal torsion bars. The 993 then gained an entirely new rear suspension with five links on each side, designed to control camber change and toe-in much more closely and further tame the tail during snap changes in throttle position.

The 996 and the 997 continue with the 993 layout in principle, although all the dimensions have changed and various trick differentials and stability systems developed over the years keep the oversteer demon at bay.

faster than is possible in the 1965 911 (that's once you've mastered the at first bewilderingly narrow and subtly misaligned shift pattern), it has all the emotional charge of a Tesco checkout scanner by comparison. Nailing the gearchange is just one of the things that cements the bond with the old-timer and makes it such an interesting thing to interact with: that unique melding of vice, virtue and simplicity carries a fascination out of all proportion to the constituent traits.

Driving Otto's car it's easy to see why people got so hooked on the 911. Its steering is lower geared and, initially, feels hopelessly vague compared with that of the Carrera S. But after a few hairpins and sweepers, you realise

it possesses a sensual subtlety that resolves kickback not so much as a tugging at the rim but a three-dimensional road map. The nerve endings in your fingertips tingle with the small but critical inputs. The surface of the road is so easy to read – the rim jiggles and writhes, alive with useful feedback. Yes, there's some initial understeer, but try harder and almost perfect balance emerges from its shadow. There's so much pure feel it's difficult to think of any other car that's as immediately addictive to drive. Or, indeed, another engine that takes such complete control of the small hairs on the back of your neck.

No, it doesn't have anything like the straight-line steam of the modern car, but neither would

'For mind-blitzing pace that can put a fast bike in its place, this year's model is a formidable tool'

	1965 911	CARRERA S
Engine	Flat-six	Flat-six
Location	Rear, longitudinal	Rear, longitudinal
Displacement	1991cc	3800cc
Bore x stroke	80 x 66mm	102 x 77.5mm
Cylinder block	Aluminium alloy, dry sump	Aluminium alloy, dry sump
Cylinder head	Aluminium alloy, sohc per bank, two valves per cylinder	Aluminium alloy, dohc per bank, four valves per cylinder VarioCam Plus
Fuel and ignition	Twin triple-choke 40PI Solex carburettors	Electronic engine management, direct fuel injection
Max power	130bhp @ 6100rpm	380bhp @ 6500rpm
Max torque	128lb ft @ 4200rpm	310lb ft @ 4400rpm
Transmission	Five-speed manual, rear-wheel drive	Seven-speed automated manual gearbox, rear-wheel drive, PSM
Front suspension	MacPherson struts, lower wishbones, torsion bar, dampers, anti-roll bar	MacPherson struts, coil springs, PASM dampers, anti-roll bar
Rear suspension	Semi-trailing arms, torsion bars, dampers	Multi-link, coil springs, PASM dampers, anti-roll bar
Brakes	Solid discs, 282mm front, 290mm rear	Vented and cross-drilled discs, 330mm front and rear, ABS, ABD
Wheels	4.5 x 15in front and rear, aluminium alloy	8 x 19in front, 11 x 19in rear, aluminium alloy
Tyres	165-HR15 front and rear	235/35 ZR19 front, 295/30 ZR19 rear
Weight (kerb)	1080kg	1455kg
Power-to-weight	122bhp/ton	265bhp/ton
0-62mph	8.5sec (claimed)	4.3sec (claimed)
Max speed	130mph (claimed)	186mph (claimed)
Basic price	c£3000 (1965)	£72,698
evo RATING	★★★★★	★★★★½

Ferdinand Porsche never got to witness the greatness the cars bearing his name would achieve; he died in 1951 and now rests in the family grave at Zell am See (above)

you believe it has just 130bhp. It feels genuinely brisk, with a real taste for the 7000rpm red line and a decently crisp response to throttle inputs. In short, it feels light and lithe and organic in a way the 2008 911 doesn't. For pure enjoyment and involvement on these roads, you'd choose it every time. For the kind of mind-blitzing pace that can put a fast bike in its place – at one point a fat-tyred Yamaha tries it on with Otto (an accomplished 917 racer) while he's driving the Carrera S and comes off worst – this year's model is a formidable tool.

When we stop to swap again, Otto's shrug is telling. 'I got bored,' he says. That would be just fine for some: massive speed and ability at your fingertips, bravery not required. It's a measure of just how far the 911 has come. It's a terrific car. But some of the magic has gone and don't let anyone, Porsche included, tell you otherwise. ■

CHANGING UP

Getrag built the gearboxes for early 911s to Porsche's design, using Porsche's own split-ring synchromesh, which was efficient but could need a hefty push on the lever. The 901 transmission (named after Porsche's internal designation for the 911) fitted in our early car has a dog-leg first gear to the left and back and the upper four gears in a conventional H-pattern, a configuration long since out of fashion although better for racing because there are fewer cross-gate movements once out of first.

As 911s gained more power, they needed a stronger gearbox, so the 915 'box arrived, in both four- and five-speed form, the latter with the modern shift pattern. As with the 901, you could have a Sportomatic transmission, which replaced the clutch with a torque converter to create a semi-automatic. It was not popular, unsurprisingly, and the late-1980s G50 gearbox, stronger and with new Borg-Warner synchromesh for a greatly improved shift action, had no Sportomatic option.

And with the 1989 arrival of the Tiptronic, offered on the new 964, there was no need. Here, Porsche invented the push-pull manual lever with which to override a full, ZF-made, torque-converter auto, and sharpened up the shifting process to suit. No true 911 enthusiast would be seen dead with a Tiptronic, though.

Now the Tiptronic is dead. In its place comes the Porsche Doppelkupplungsgetriebe, or double-clutch gearbox, or PDK. What most of us call a DSG has seemingly come late to Porsche, but actually the company invented the idea and used it in the 956 race car 25 years ago. It has seven speeds and three shift-speed modes, the fastest of which has an abruptness thus far alien to the DSG idea.

Seven optimum gear ratios and close control of throttle-blips makes a PDK 911 'officially' more economical than a manual one. A further nail in the coffin of the conventional manual transmission? Use it or lose it, you might say.

Original 911 turbo concept of 1973 spawned two cars – 930 Turbo road car (left) and 2.1-litre RSR Turbo race-car (above) with up to 500bhp

Birth of an icon

1974
Porsche 911 Turbo

It's late 1973 and we're in the depths of an oil crisis. A 60mph speed limit has been imposed in Germany, including the Nürburgring and Porsche's own Weissach test track. Not the best time to be planning the launch of your fastest ever road car...

Porsche is on a high, though. Its outrageous 1100bhp turbocharged 917/30 sports racer has dominated the CanAm championship in the US, and the company has accumulated a wealth of experience of turbocharging air-cooled engines. It is only logical that it should transfer that knowledge to its famous tail-engined sports car. And so, at the 1973 Paris motor show, it unveils a prototype turbocharged 911. Question is, will they dare put it into production?

In fact two cars came out of that Paris prototype. The first was the 2.1-litre Martini 911 RSR Turbo, the second, Type 930.

Porsche was being run at the time by Ernst Fuhrmann, the engineer behind the early 356 flat-four engine; even as Porsche MD he was always happy to roll his sleeves up and get the spanners out. Fuhrmann also had balls, and decided that the 911 Turbo project should go ahead.

However, then triggered a huge argument within Porsche management as to what sort of car it should be. One school reckoned it should be a stripped-out high-performance 911; the other proposed that it should be a well-equipped and sophisticated flagship for the entire Porsche range. The sales department, understandably jittery at the thought of trying to sell a highly expensive sports car when people were queuing for petrol, wanted a car with the lowest price possible.

Fuhrmann was in the flagship camp, as was company finance director Heinz Branitzki. 'If we can't sell a machine as good as the 911 Turbo,' Branitzki declared, 'then we should get out of the sports car business.'

Companies that are small – like Porsche was in the early 1970s – with a deep involvement in racing and a decisive leader, work quickly. By the spring of 1974, engineers Herbert Ampferer and Heinz Dorsch had tested both 2.7 and 3-litre engines. The 3-litre motor was chosen because it gave the most torque low down. Porsche had discovered with the 917's flat-12 that the bigger it was in capacity, the smoother the transition from off to on-boost running.

Modern turbo engines run compression ratios not far off that of naturally aspirated engines but, in the days before sophisticated engine management systems, ratios had to be kept low to prevent detonation. Porsche had the added problem of air-cooling, so the ratio was pinned to a conservative 6.5:1. The crankcase, steel crank and rods were standard, but both cylinder barrels and cylinder heads were bespoke pieces designed to manage extreme combustion temperatures – including sodium-filled exhaust valves. As well as a conventional wastegate, the 930 engine had a blow-off valve fitted to the induction manifold which allowed the turbo's turbines to keep spinning. (Such a valve had been used successfully on the CanAm cars.)

Test engines gave at least 280bhp, but because the boost came in suddenly and dramatically it was decided that the car would be too much of a handful in inexperienced hands, so the power was pegged back to 260bhp. This, though, in a car that weighed only 1140kg.

Porsche took its standard 915 transaxle and seriously beefed it up for the 930 Turbo. Only four speeds were fitted, which had the benefit of freeing up space inside the casing for larger and stronger gears. The gearbox had a torque capacity of 475lb ft, which was more than strong enough for the road car and tough enough for racing, too.

The 911 Turbo was shown at the Paris show in autumn 1974 and, not surprisingly in an era when turbocharging was extremely exotic, captivated the world's motoring press. Porsche had its first supercar.

If you're under 40 it's difficult to appreciate the effect the arrival of the 911 Turbo had on car enthusiasts of all ages. No schoolboy bedroom wall was complete without an Athena poster of the 930 Turbo – complete with Pirelli P7 tyres with a profile lower than anything we'd ever seen before.